EVANGELIZATION AND CATECHESIS

Evangelization and Catechesis

by
Johannes Hofinger, S.J.

PAULIST PRESS
New York/Paramus/Toronto

Cum Permissu Superiorum

NIHIL OBSTAT
James C. Turro
Censor Librorum

✠ IMPRIMATUR
Most Rev. Peter L. Gerety, D.D.
Archbishop of Newark

January 5, 1976

Library of Congress
Catalog Card Number: 75-36171

ISBN: 0-8091-1928-5

Published by Paulist Press
Editorial Office: 1865 Broadway, N.Y., N.Y. 10023
Business Office: 400 Sette Drive, Paramus, N.J. 07652

Printed and bound in the
United States of America

Contents

To
Alfonso M. Nebreda, S.J.

Preface

The manuscript of this book was almost finished when the news of the death of Father Josef Jungmann, S.J., reached me. He died in Innsbruck, Austria, on January 26, 1975.

It was almost forty years ago that my great teacher and fatherly friend put to the men of his time the question "Do we really proclaim the Gospel?" His book, *Die Frohbotschaft und unsere Glaubensverkündigung (The Good News and Our Proclamation of the Faith)*, was published in 1936.

As is well known, Father Jungmann's book led at that time to a most fruitful renewal of catechesis. Yet the same question needs to be advanced again today in a religious situation which differs very greatly from that in which he wrote.

Throughout the world nowadays, we hear heartfelt complaints about the ineffectiveness of catechesis and of all kinds of Christian preaching. We face a widespread lack of interest in religion among Christian people of all ages and situations.

Until recently many experts and leaders thought that the failure of catechesis and preaching in our times came primarily from a lack of contact with modern man—an inability to understand his vital problems, his mentality, his very language. There cannot be any doubt that often we did not take modern man and his special problems seriously enough. That must be corrected.

But could it not also be true that we did not sufficiently understand Jesus Christ and his aim in proclaiming the Gospel, that we did not approach modern man with the true attitude of Christ? Could it not be that we did not care enough to ask ourselves, first of all, what the Gospel demands of us, the "evangelists," if we and our message are to be accepted by men today?

The 1974 Synod of Bishops, which had as its theme "the evangelization of the modern world," aroused new interest in this topic. It has led to a valuable reassessment of the religious situation which the preaching of the Gospel confronts in today's world. But has the Synod really led men to the necessary awareness of the deeper causes why our proclamation of the Gospel is often shallow and ineffective?

The present book does not pretend to give definitive answers to the pressing questions that it places. We will have to content ourselves with arousing interest in these questions and in pointing to the basic principles necessary for any satisfactory answer.

In preparing this manuscript I have been generously helped by my friend, Father Richard Maughan. I owe him thanks not only for making the book presentable to the reader, but also for many pertinent suggestions in regard to its content.

New Orleans
Pentecost, 1975

Chapter One
Meaning and Importance
of Evangelization

Two shocking facts are, or should be, causing great shame to Christians in today's world. The first is that two thousand years after the coming of Christ, the vast majority of men still do not know him or, at least, do not expect anything from him.

The second and even more shameful fact consists in our own poor response to the Christ event. The vast majority of those who profess to be Christians are not really committed to Christ and his Gospel. In fact, they live as if Jesus had never come into the world.

How can we explain these two facts reasonably? There can be no satisfactory explanation unless we sincerely admit our own unsatisfactory proclamation of Christ's Gospel. We must consider the fact of insufficient evangelization.

The Role of Evangelization
in God's Plan of Salvation

Before God, in the fullness of time, sent us his own Son, he prepared mankind through many other messengers for this decisive event in his relationship with man. The great leaders and prophets of the Old Testament were, above all, the great messengers of hope, the heralds of the coming salvation. Then Christ himself came in order to proclaim to his brothers and sisters the love of his and our Father in heaven and to bring us the fullness of God's love with his work of redemption.

According to God's plan of salvation, Christ came for all

3

men. God has given his Son to all of us to be the teacher and savior of all. God "wants everyone to be saved and reach full knowledge of the truth. For there is only one God, and there is only one mediator between God and mankind, himself a man, Christ Jesus, who sacrificed himself as a ransom for all of them. He is the evidence of this, sent at the appointed time" (1 Tm. 2:4ff).

Christ died and rose again "to gather together the scattered children of God" (Jn. 11:52). "He came to bring the good news of peace, peace to you who were far away and peace to those who were near at hand. Through him, both of us have in the one Spirit our way to come to the Father" (Eph. 2:17f).

In his ineffable love God has planned not only the individual salvation of each man who accepts his loving invitation, but also the salvation of the whole human community and, together with man, of the whole world. It was the plan of God that he "would bring everything together under Christ as head, everything in the heavens and everything on earth" (Eph. 1:10; see also Rom. 8:19-23; 1 Cor. 15:20-28).

Because God loves us, he takes us seriously, according to the human nature which he himself planned with so much love and called into existence. God does not contradict himself in his works. A magical kind of salvation or a salvation forced upon man, conferred on him without his consent and his active collaboration, would not be a gift but rather an offense to man, who is intelligent and free.

If God in his love invites man to a union of life and love with him, man must know about that intention of God and must ratify it with his own free and firm commitment. To bring man the good news of God's loving intention, to make him aware of this unique opportunity and to animate him to accept the invitation of God and commit himself to a life in accordance with that invitation—that is precisely the true meaning of evangelization.

To evangelize means to proclaim the love of God which comes to us through Christ Jesus, and to proclaim it in such a manner that man, with the grace of God, accepts it with his own free and firm commitment.

Coming as he did after the long preparation of the Old Testament, Christ was the first to bring us the good news of God's plan of salvation. It was he who first proclaimed God's saving love in this new and decisive way. It was he who first challenged us to make a radical change in our lives in response to God's love.

But there is evidence that Christ during his public life did not yet explain God's saving plan in any detail. Even his most intimate disciples came to understand it only in the light of their paschal and pentecostal experience. Jesus, it is true, charged his disciples with the proclamation of the good news (cf., e.g., Mt. 28:16-20; Mk. 16:15-18; Jn. 20:21). But at the same time he made it clear that they could do so appropriately only with the help of the Holy Spirit whom he would send to them (cf. Jn. 14:26, 16:12f; Lk. 24:49). In fact, the good news of our salvation through Jesus Christ was understood and proclaimed for the first time in virtue of the pentecostal grace and experience of the apostles.

In this way evangelization is a constitutive element in God's plan of salvation; it is decidedly the work of the Holy Spirit, and that not only in its beginnings at Pentecost. This will be so until the Lord comes again in glory to terminate this work of evangelization. It is the "Spirit of truth" who gives the disciples of Christ the right understanding of the Gospel. Moreover, it is the Holy Spirit who instills in them the apostolic vigor and enables them to substantiate their proclamation with the convincing proofs of God's presence and assistance.

The Holy Spirit works not only in the one who proclaims the good news but also in those who listen. He opens their hearts from within. He animates them to accept the Gospel. He stimulates them to commit themselves wholeheartedly. With good reason, the last Synod of Bishops insisted upon this decisive role of the Holy Spirit in the work of evangelization. Whenever those who proclaim the Gospel do not appreciate the interior action of the Holy Spirit and do not count on it in their proclamation, grave shortcomings result in the work of evangelization.

From the beginning evangelization has been understood

and carried out as an ecclesial activity and not just the private enterprise of some individual enthusiasts. The Holy Spirit formed the primitive Christian community. The first Christians proclaimed the Gospel as members of the community; they invited and led their converts to a new life within that community, and the whole community recognized the pastoral and doctrinal authority of those whom Christ in a very special way had charged with the proclamation of the Gospel and the care of the community.

In the New Testament we find two forms of proclaiming the Gospel. The first is the proclamation of God's saving plan to people who do not yet know it. The objective is to lead them to an initial Christian commitment and to integrate them into the Christian community. This was accomplished by the sacrament of baptism.

But after baptism, the formation of the neophytes continued; they had to strengthen themselves in their faith and in the Christian life. In this way the pastoral testament of Christ, as we find it in Matthew 28:16-20, distinguishes between pre-baptismal catechesis ("Go, therefore, and make disciples of all nations; baptize them . . .") and instruction after baptism ("and teach them to observe all the commandments . . .").

In his narration of the pentecostal event, Luke presents first the talk of Peter which prepared the people for and invited them to baptism (Acts 2:14-39). But immediately after telling of the baptism of the first Christians, Luke underlines the fact that they received further instruction from the apostles (Acts 2:42).

In a similar manner religious educators in recent times, under the influence of mission catechetics, have with good reason made a distinction. The first proclamation of the Gospel, which leads to an initial commitment of faith, has been called evangelization. The religious formation that follows, dealing with Christians who are basically committed, has been called catechesis.

In order to clarify the aim of the present study, it may be worthwhile to examine in somewhat more detail the reasons for this distinction and to determine precisely how the word "evangelization" is understood in this book.

"Evangelization and Catechesis"
or "Evangelizing Catechesis"?

In recent years, not a few national centers and diocesan departments of religious education, especially in Latin America, changed their official designation, preferring to be called centers and departments of "evangelization and catechesis." By this change they obviously intended to put special emphasis on evangelization and to assign it the first place in the ministry of the word. Many agree that this wholesome stress on evangelization has come rather late.

The change in emphasis, however, is easily understood in the light of the present pastoral situation. There is a multitude of baptized Christians but only a limited number of Christians who really live their commitment to Christ. We have also had to face the incontestable fact that many Christians, who receive in one way or another rather intensive religious instruction, obtain little profit from it for their Christian life for the simple reason that this instruction lacks an evangelizing dimension.

Despite this new emphasis on evangelization, praiseworthy as it is, the "evangelists" themselves are not always clear about what evangelization really means and about its demands on the ministry of the word today. In meetings of religious teachers, including priests and religious, the following questions are being asked with surprising frequency: "What does evangelization finally mean? How does it differ from ordinary catechesis? What is its place in the whole process of religious education?"

The word "evangelization" in fact is being given a variety of meanings in books now being published. In order to avoid confusion, we must therefore make clear our meaning in this study.

Although the General Catechetical Directory does not define evangelization, it gives a quite adequate description of its special function in the whole process of religious formation. "Catechesis proper," according to the Directory, "presupposes a global adherence to Christ's Gospel as presented by the Church. Often, however, it is directed to men who, though they belong to the Church, have never in fact given a personal adherence to the message of revelation" (no. 18) and therefore need special help by which they can be guided to their first real commitment of faith.

If we understand evangelization in this way, we are presented with a very clear distinction between evangelization and catechesis. Evangelization comprises efforts which prepare and —with due respect to man's freedom and God's undeserved grace—bring into being the first responsible adherence to the Gospel of Christ on the part of the person to be catechized.

Catechesis, on the other hand, comprises all efforts intended to make man's first commitment of faith become ever more living, conscious and active through the light of instruction (no. 17).

According to the General Catechetical Directory all catechetical activity has to "lead both communities and individual members of the faithful to maturity of faith" (no. 21). In the process of religious formation, evangelization is the initial stage by which man is led, step by step, to his first true commitment of faith.

By that commitment "man entrusts his whole self freely to God, offering the full submission of intellect and will to God who reveals" (*Constitution on Divine Revelation*, no. 5). The subsequent catechesis has to lead to an ever greater maturity of that initial and global commitment of faith. This last is the function of catechesis "proper."

For the past twenty years, leaders of missionary catechesis like André Liege, O.P., and Alfonso Nebreda, S.J., have distinguished evangelization from catechesis. They have rightly insisted upon the fundamental importance of the first commitment of faith and upon the great difference between the instruction and guidance which leads to the first act of faith and the following catechetical instruction which brings the initial faith to its maturity.

This definition of and distinction between evangelization and catechesis may be logically clear, but they include practical difficulties. If we understand evangelization and catechesis as two clearly distinct phases of the whole process of religious formation, we obviously need another simple and accepted word for the whole work of religious instruction and formation. As yet, we do not in fact have one.

And because we lack it, the word "catechesis" continues to be used—even in the best catechetical literature of our times, including the General Catechetical Directory (see, e.g., nn. 18 and 21)—to describe the entire process whereby one is guided to mature faith.

The new insistence upon evangelization originated from a thorough analysis of missionary preaching and of religious instruction of adults who, although having been baptized, had never come to a true Christian commitment. In such cases, as all agree, evangelization can be distinguished from the catechesis proper which follows.

But such a distinction is much more difficult—even impossible—to maintain in the catechesis of children. Considering the fact that children, because of their natural immaturity, are still incapable of a true commitment of faith, we have to consider the catechesis of children to be a form of pre-evangelization, that is, a preparation for their first fully responsible act of faith. On the other hand, taking into account their basic willingness to accept the message of Christ, we have to consider the religious instruction of such children as catechesis proper.

Even in the religious instruction of adult Christians, it is often difficult to distinguish clearly between evangelization and catechesis. The commitment of faith admits of very different degrees of perfection, and for this reason it is difficult to make a neat and clear distinction between those who need basic evangelization and those, basically initiated, who need ongoing catechesis.

In practice, we work with groups where almost all have some basic faith. It would be quite difficult, however, to determine who and how many have already committed themselves to a truly Christian life. Yet it is easy to see that practically all need a thorough revitalization of their faith.

For this reason the best catechetical literature of today no longer insists very strongly upon a neat distinction between evangelization and catechesis as two different phases of the whole process of formation. The General Catechetical Directory explicitly declares that in practice evangelization and catechesis cannot be neatly separated, but rather have to accompany and supplement one another.

"According to circumstances," the Directory says, "evangelization can precede and accompany the work of catechesis proper. In every case, however, one must keep in mind that the element of conversion is always present in the dynamism of faith, and for that reason any form of catechesis must also perform the role of evangelization" (no. 18). What really counts is the evangelizing dimension of all religious instruction, not evangelization and catechesis stressed as two different activities.

Also significant is the way evangelization is understood in the text that the Holy See presented as a "working tool" for the preparation of the 1974 Synod of Bishops which dealt with evangelization. The term "evangelization" was understood as "the activity whereby the Gospel is proclaimed and explained, and whereby living faith is awakened in non-Christians and fostered in Christians (missionary preaching, catechetics, homiletics, etc.)," or, somewhat more briefly, "the activity whereby the Church proclaims the Gospel so that faith may be aroused, may unfold and may grow" (*The Evangelization of the Modern World*, United States Catholic Conference, Washington, 1973, pp. 1f).

This is exactly the meaning in which the term "evangelization" is used in this book. In other words it is not understood as that particular phase of catechetical activity that precedes ordinary catechesis; it means rather that indispensable quality of any authentic catechesis which arouses faith and unfolds it in those being catechized.

We might call it the evangelizing dimension of catechesis. According to this use of "evangelization," we could then say that a catechesis evangelizes to the extent that it leads others to faith, be it that first commitment of faith or its further deepening and maturation.

The main reason for using this definition of the word "evangelization" is found in the particular purpose of this book. It is addressed to all heralds of God's word, priests and catechists alike, and is meant to serve them in their efforts to make all catechetical activity a true proclamation of the Gospel.

The major defect in the catechesis of the past was, after all, not the lack of a clear distinction between the first proclamation of the Gospel and the catechesis which followed, although this distinction also was important. The problem rather consisted in the fact that catechetical activity as a whole so often lacked the necessary evangelical dimension. And in many cases, this is still true today.

It is the special aim of this book to show clearly just what this evangelical dimension of catechesis involves and also what it requires from preachers and catechists in their work.

In using this term "evangelization" in the broader meaning of the Fourth Synod of Bishops, we do not in any way want to minimize the great importance of the initial proclamation of the Gospel and the particular function and method which distinguishes it from the catechesis that must follow.

In a pastoral situation such as we have today, we must do everything possible to lead the countless Christians who have never given themselves to Christ as their first commitment of faith. This groundwork of evangelization will not have any real lasting result, however, if the whole catechetical process is not carefully planned, arranged and carried out in a way that renews and deepens ever more fully that initial—and, by its nature, imperfect—commitment.

How evangelization ought in practice to accompany and complement catechesis can best be seen from the following principles of genuine evangelizing catechesis.

Some Basic Principles of Evangelizing Catechesis

What follow are some basic norms designed to insure the evangelizing dimension of the entire ministry of the word.

1. *All catechetical activity must aim at the commitment of faith.* The strategies may differ in different kinds of catechetical activity—preparing more indirectly for the first commitment in pre-evangelization; soliciting the first true commitment of faith in evangelization proper; consolidating and deepening it in cat-

echesis proper. In each of these the strategies may differ, but without exception they must ultimately be directed toward the commitment of faith.

Any religious instruction which only transmits information about religion without that purposeful orientation to the commitment of faith does not deserve to be called catechesis. This does not mean, however, that each kind of catechesis has to foster the commitment of faith in the same way.

There is surely an important place for a "didascalia," i.e., for a catechesis which explains the various doctrines of faith in more detail, presenting their deep religious meaning in a truly Christian way of life. But such catechesis already supposes a basic commitment of faith; it must never consist merely in relaying information to satisfy religious curiosity without enlightening, inspiring and motivating the life of faith.

2. *Any catechesis which supposes an initial commitment of faith before those to be catechized have in fact committed themselves will end in failure.* The most decisive question in giving religious instruction is not whether those whom we address can understand it—though this, too, is obviously very important! The question is whether listeners are disposed to accept the message in an attitude of faith. If this attitude is missing, we will surely "speak to the walls."

Especially in the case of students who have been ordered to receive religious instruction, we should expect nothing from such instruction unless we first secure a necessary positive disposition on the part of the students. The more catechesis deals with the details of the Christian message, the more it requires a solid foundation on which faith can build.

3. *The first commitment of faith cannot be taken for granted.* In the present pastoral situation, it cannot be supposed that even a majority of the Christians who regularly participate in the life of the Church have ever really understood their Christian commitment. Their religious practice may result from a traditional, legalistic religious behavior without any true faith commitment. Many Christians are lacking not in good will but in the kind of solid religious formation geared to more solid commitment.

The mere fact that teenagers, for example, come from traditionally Catholic families or that they have received their education in Catholic schools does not guarantee true commitment of faith. Many teenagers lose the immature faith of their childhood and abandon interest in all things religious. Quite often they do not appreciate the religious education they received; they may even harbor a resentment against religion itself.

In such cases it is harmful if parents or other authorities insist that these adolescents be given a detailed exposition of the mysteries of faith without providing the catechist with the opportunity to lay the necessary foundation. What such teenagers need is evangelization proper, but not without a "pre-evangelization," adapted, of course, to their special circumstances. And while such efforts at "pre-evangelization" ought not to lose precious time, they should not, on the other hand, try to hurry religious commitment too sharply.

4. *In a concrete case the catechist must always take into account the religious situation of the majority of his group.* The catechist must adapt himself as much as possible to the special needs of a group. When we form small groups of committed Christians—*communidades de base* as they are known in Latin America—we usually begin with some solid evangelization according to special needs. But even in more traditional settings, we should try to provide programs of evangelization for Christian adults who until now have never really appreciated their faith and never understood the true meaning of Christian commitment.

For this, the weeks of Lent may be the most convenient time. Provided that the program is varied from year to year, it will also be of great help to the committed Christian in renewing and deepening commitment. Care must be taken, however, to gear the program to those who need most to be awakened to a true life of faith.

Every kind of religious formation must, in sum, be adapted to the human and religious level of those being taught—never requiring a perfection of commitment which surpasses their psychological capacity (catechesis of children!) and never supposing a religious level or interest which in the majority of the group is still lacking.

5. *We should never remain satisfied with the first true commitment of faith.* However sincere and deep it may be, an initial commitment by its very nature requires continuous renewal and deepening. The maturation of the initial faith is the aim of all subsequent catechesis.

We shall deal with the gradual maturation of faith and the way to achieve it in more detail in the following chapter. There we shall see that faith matures by a simultaneous and balanced growth in two dimensions. The ever-deepening understanding of the content of faith must be accompanied by a corresponding ever-deeper commitment of faith.

6. *In order to achieve the right equilibrium between religious understanding and adherence in the growth of faith, good catechesis must distinguish itself by being:*

Substantial, that is, properly emphasizing the main elements of God's message of salvation. "In the message of salvation there is a certain hierarchy of truths which the Church has always recognized when it composed creeds or summaries of truths of faith. On all levels catechesis should take account of this hierarchy of truths of faith" (General Catechetical Directory, no. 43).

Existential, presenting lucidly the meaning of the particular doctrines in relation to true Christian life, and thus showing clearly the inner connection of these doctrines with the very meaning of our Christian commitment.

7. *Preference must be given to evangelizing catechesis and not to ritualistic sacramentalism.* Any tendency to substitute for the basic evangelization a kind of ritualistic sacramentalism that lacks a true commitment of faith is a pastoral blunder; it contradicts equally the Gospel and all apostolic tradition.

Only through authentic evangelization can we lead people to a true appreciation, reception and realization of the sacraments set within the context of the Christian life. Those who ask for the sacraments, without being willing to accept the necessary sacramental catechesis, are in danger of reducing the sacraments to little more than a valuable old cultural tradition or means for a magical kind of salvation.

The principles we have presented here will be clarified and substantiated more fully in the chapters to follow.

Chapter Two
Faith: The Objective
of Evangelization

Whoever lacks a sense of time and does not appreciate it cannot appreciate a watch; the only function of the watch consists in indicating the time. In the same way, whoever does not understand what faith really is and does not appreciate it cannot understand what evangelization is. Nor can he appreciate it, since the only purpose of evangelization consists in transmitting authentic faith.

By using this comparison, we have, however, intimated a great difference between the two situations. A watch only indicates time; it cannot bring or transmit time. Evangelization, on the other hand, not only indicates faith but also transmits it —or, more correctly, it imparts, deepens and perfects faith.

Evangelization cannot, of course, give faith. Faith comes always from God's own action within us and from the free decision of the man who believes. Evangelization has only instrumental causality in transmitting faith; it is our instrumental contribution to the service of God. God makes use of us in order to lead those whom we evangelize to authentic faith and to let them grow and mature in it. Thus we come to the decisive question.

What Does Authentic Faith Mean?

The best way to undestand what faith really means is to see it as man's response to the loving invitation of God who reveals. This is exactly the way that Scripture and Vatican II present it.

John the Evangelist pertinently summarizes the Christian experience which we transmit to our brothers when he says: "We ourselves have known and put our faith in God's love toward ourselves. God is love, and anyone who lives in love lives in God and God lives in him" (1 Jn. 4:16).

"The obedience of faith (Rom. 16:26; cf. Rom. 1:5; 2 Cor. 10:5-6) must be given to God who reveals, an obedience by which man entrusts his whole self to God, offering the full submission of intellect and will" (*Constitution on Divine Revelation*, no. 5). By this text, as we know, the Council intended to correct a too intellectual presentation of faith which had characterized much of pre-conciliar theology and catechesis.

In the period before the Council, even the classical definition of faith, prominent in the vast majority of catechisms, insisted too strongly upon the intellectual aspect. "Faith," we learned from these catechisms, "is the divine virtue by which we assent to the truths revealed by God, since God cannot deceive or be deceived."

Well, what faculty does man use to assent to truths? Obviously it is his intellect. The will, it is true, may influence this intellectual assent; nevertheless, the assent to truths as such is clearly an intellectual act. The answer of the catechism reflected the predominant trend in pre-conciliar theology.

This school of theology presented divine revelation too much as a system of "eternal truths" revealed by God so that, by accepting them with due submission of our intellect, we acknowledge his authority. This sort of thought found its characteristic expression in the very definition which many textbooks of dogmatic theology gave for revelation: "Locutio Dei attestans," meaning an authoritative communication from God. In this communication—the professors then went on to explain to their theology students—God communicates to us his ideas in order that we may assent to them as true in the act of faith.

But divine revelation looks quite different if, with Vatican II, we consider it as God's loving invitation. In divine revelation, the Council tells us, "the invisible God, out of the abundance of his love, speaks to men as friends (cf. Ex. 33:11; Jn. 15:14-15) and lives among them (cf. Bar. 3:38), so that he may invite them and take them into fellowship with himself" (*Constitution on Divine Revelation*, no. 2).

What God intends by his revelation is, above all, to establish a union of love and life with man. Therefore, he manifests his plan of salvation and challenges man to enter into a deep and lasting friendship with him. To accept this challenge of the Divine Lover, man answers with his "yes" of faith.

An invitation cannot, of course, be meaningfully accepted before it is sufficiently understood. The intellect, therefore, also has an important and irreplaceable role to play in our response of faith. But the "yes" which finally counts and by which someone accepts an invitation is, after all, the free decision of the invited person.

And that holds true especially in this case. God challenges man to make a fundamental option which gives to his whole life a new meaning and a new orientation. This unique invitation opens to man new and unthought of dimensions in his existence. Yet, at the same time, it demands from man a total surrender and a final commitment. The Council does not deny that the response of faith includes an assent of the intellect; it only wants to stress that the act of faith is more than that. It requires a total surrender to God: "Man entrusts his whole self freely to God."

In order to avoid any misunderstanding, it may be worthwhile to mention explicitly that whenever we speak in this book, and most especially in this chapter, about the nature of faith, we speak always of actual faith or the act of faith, and not of what theologians used to call "infused" faith. Infused faith means the exigency and capacity for actual faith. It is God's gift which we received together with his life in baptism. By itself it does not give the psychological facility of faith. Much less can it ever actualize itself automatically. From the catechetical point of view, "infused" faith can be disregarded without any risk, provided that we keep ourselves aware of the fundamental principle that the act of faith cannot be produced by the catechist.

We find the role of the catechist in the education of faith well-formulated in the General Catechetical Directory. The catechist, it says, "is responsible for choosing and creating conditions which are necessary for the Christian message to be sought, accepted and more profoundly investigated. This is the point to which the action of the catechist extends—and there it stops. For adherence on the part of those to be taught is a fruit of grace and freedom, and does not depend on the catechist; and catechetical action, therefore, should be accompanied by prayer" (no. 71).

To this loving invitation of God, man answers by actual faith. This does not, of course, imply that God can be satisfied by some sporadic acts of faith. The divine revelation challenges us to a life of friendship with God. Such a challenge can only be accepted by a decision that gives to our lives a new and permanent orientation toward God as our Lord and Divine Lover.

As in any true friendship, what counts in our friendship with God far more than any particular acts considered in themselves are our basic attitude and orientation toward him as the very meaning of our lives. Particular acts have value only insofar as they are rooted in this fundamental attitude, and insofar as they manifest and deepen it. What God expects from his beloved children is a life of faith which in the totality of its free acts responds to his loving invitation.

The personal communication which God has in mind when he reveals himself to man is aptly characterized by the Council as true friendship. However, we must never forget the uniqueness of this relationship. If we do not insist upon the very special character of such friendship, it will be greatly misunderstood. It must never be thought of as just one of the many friendships we find in our lives.

The Divine Lover claims first place in our hearts and lives and he is not willing to share this place with anyone. The Bible is most forceful in speaking of this primacy of God. "If anyone comes to me without hating his father, mother, wife, children, brothers, sisters, yes, and his own life too, he cannot be my disciple" (Lk. 4:26).

Obviously, the Lord does not demand a rupture of these loving relationships which God the Creator himself founded and requires by his commandments. What Christ wants emphatically to express is simply that the first place is always due to God in our lives. The friendship with God does not exclude other relationships of true and deep love, but it must be allowed to rule, purify and coordinate all of them.

Our friendship with God must also not be misunderstood as a friendship with someone whom we can meet on an equal level. The tenderness of God's love must not blind us to his transcendence and lordship. In the catechesis of young people especially, we must take care that the friendship of God is clearly distinguished from early friendships in their lives.

And, finally, man's friendship with God is in the moral sense an obligatory friendship. Here we have another aspect of our friendship with God that is often misunderstood. Every friendship is by its very nature psychologically free insofar as we have the psychological freedom to accept or refuse it. A forced friendship is a contradiction. Yet just as the love, kindness and sacrifices of our parents oblige us to a response of filial love and gratitude, so the infinite love and goodness of God obliges us much more to accept gratefully the challenge of his invitation.

When God invites us to friendship with him, he expects us to accept his challenge with a commitment of loyalty and love. And this commitment of acceptance is exactly what we mean by faith. No other friendship requires and deserves so dedicated and profound a commitment as our loving union with God. Authentic faith is, in fact, the deepest and firmest commitment in human life.

The reader must have noticed, and probably with some surprise, that in this section on authentic faith we have spoken incessantly of love. It is the Council which has forced us to do this. The identity of faith and love is an inevitable result of its teaching on revelation and faith.

We have always held the intimate connections between faith and love and have insisted that faith must lead to love, but we have not identified them in this way. If faith is understood, as in pre-conciliar theology, to be our intellectual assent to God's word, such faith logically requires the love of this God who is so good and great. But an act of love is not yet included. Many men, indeed, content themselves with merely intellectual faith. Without any hesitation they accept all revealed doctrine as true, but at the same time they do not commit themselves in any way. On the other hand, one who with Vatican II considers authentic faith to be the committed acceptance of God's invitation—an invitation by which God urges us to true friendship with him—must in consequence describe faith with the Council as an act of total surrender. And that obviously means love. In such a case faith and love are only two different aspects of one and the same saving reality.

Genuine faith, as Scripture and the Council describe it, already includes love and therefore justifies. It consists by its nature in the committed acceptance of the whole plan of salvation. By his act of faith, man commits himself sincerely to give whatever God may expect of him.

It is obvious that this conciliar understanding of faith will help us immensely in our brotherly dialogue with Protestants. It provides us with the correct understanding of that famous and controversial saying—"faith alone saves." The commitment of faith does not dispense us from the rest but commits us to it.

For a fuller understanding of genuine faith and to distinguish it from defective forms and adulterations of faith, it may help to ponder the main qualities of authentic faith. This we shall do in the next section which deals with the growth of faith.

The Growth of Faith

The commitment of faith, like any commitment of trust and friendship, admits of various degrees. Evangelization must not content itself with an initial commitment of faith, necessarily still imperfect. It must always strive to bring this first commitment to maturity.

The growth and maturation of faith requires simultaneous progress on two levels. We find a pertinent statement about this in the General Catechetical Directory: "Faith, the maturing of which is to be promoted by catechesis, can be considered in two ways, either as the total adherence given by man under the influence of grace to God revealing himself (the faith *by which* one believes), or as the content of revelation or of the Christian message (the faith *which* one believes.) These two aspects are by their very nature inseparable, and a normal maturing of the faith assumes the progress of both together" (n. 36).

This basic principle may be illustrated best by the normal growth of the human body. Growing in only one direction, e.g., upward without a proportionate broadening, would be harmful. In the case of our bodies, nature takes care of the healthy growth in both directions. But in the maturation of faith, there are no built-in mechanisms that regulate growth automatically.

In this connection we should never forget that the aspect of total adherence is the more important, and that the other aspect has simply a function of service. The depth of faith definitely counts more than its extension. A Christian can reach true holiness with a faith of very limited doctrinal breadth.

Yet we must also understand that no one is dispensed by the depth of his faith from efforts to attain an ever deepening understanding of the content of faith according to his own educational possibilities. A lack of interest in the content of revelation almost always manifests a deficient commitment of faith. A son who does not make the effort to correctly understand what his father tells him is hardly distinguished by his filial commitment. Before the Council, it is true, we often overstressed the material aspect of faith, that is, the "purity" and extension of faith. But today the opposite is happening, and many people are in serious danger from the tendency to minimize this aspect of faith, for it is also necessary for a healthy growth toward faith maturity.

Growth always aims at maturity; growth of faith, therefore, must aim at attaining mature faith. But what does mature faith really mean? Many catechists cannot lead others to mature faith because they themselves do not have it and do not even know in what it consists.

Mature faith must distinguish itself by the following characteristics:

1. *It consists of an intimate personal relationship with God* as the only one who deserves the total surrender of our whole self. It must be distinguished by an emphasis upon the absolute

transcendence of God and by its entirely personal character. On the other hand, any kind of religious behavior which obscures the transcendence of God by some unbalanced devotion to saints or by some unhealthy concern for sacred objects is always a clear sign of a still immature faith.

2. *It must be reasonable.* The total surrender of faith does not mean blind faith in the sense that there are no valid human motives for entrusting ourselves to God in this way. If in any human friendship we require solid motives which justify our commitment of trust and loyalty, how much more must this be true in the commitment of faith, inasmuch as faith demands absolute surrender.

Reasonable faith also implies that the believer is clearly aware of what he believes and why he believes. Any kind of faith that loses itself in a particular doctrine and lacks a clear idea of the main thrust of God's whole revelation is still immature. The same can be said of a faith which cannot distinguish between pious opinions and doctrines clearly revealed by God— for example, between the question of the historicity of the Holy House at Loretto and the dogma of the incarnation.

The more particular doctrines are understood and evaluat-ed in the light of the central idea of Christian revelation, the more such faith is reasonable and worthy of a mature man. It is a sign of religious formation. This concentration on the main meaning and intention of God's word enables the mature Christian to distinguish clearly between more and less important doctrines of faith and prevents him from any overemphasis on peripheral doctrines to the neglect of more central truths. Such an enlightened Christian will never be in danger of concerning himself more with guardian angels than with divine providence, more with indulgences than with the spirit of repentance.

A mature Christian with a solid religious formation must be able to give solid reasons not only for his faith as a whole, for his total acceptance of the word of God as he receives it from the Church, but also for the specifics of his faith, for ex-ample, why the Church interprets the doctrine of the Eucharist in a particular manner.

A merely traditional faith, one which someone accepts

blindly from his environment, can at the very best be considered only the beginning of faith. In the strict sense, it is not yet Christian faith grounded on the authority of God, and it needs a drastic purification and deepening.

3. *It excels by the depth of its commitment.* A true friendship distinguishes itself from a flirtation by its commitment of trust, loyalty and love. A true commitment requires psychological freedom of the person who commits himself, and firmness in this free decision beyond any hesitation and vacillation.

We have already mentioned that the psychological freedom of a commitment does not exclude a true moral obligation to make it. As in all human life, psychological freedom admits of very different degrees. Maturation of faith, therefore, supposes maturation of human freedom. The firmness of faith manifests itself, above all, by its independence from unfavorable influences of one's environment which may shake and diminish faith as well as from momentary feelings and personal caprices which may hinder the actualization of faith. People who pray only when they feel like praying surely lack mature faith.

4. *It penetrates the whole life and transforms it.* Through faith we entrust ourselves to God as the fundamental cause, author, meaning and master of our existence; from him we accept a new orientation to our lives. Mature faith, therefore, must penetrate all our activity. A faith which restricts itself to certain religious customs is not worthy to be called faith. A faith which actualizes itself in occasional prayers, while failing to penetrate one's whole family life or the various professional, socio-political and recreational activities, is also still immature.

This penetration, however, is a gradual process and it requires continual deepening. Even many practicing Catholics of good will, because of their rather defective religious formation, put up with a very imperfect penetration. Sometimes they block important and vast spheres of their lives, for example, professional and social activities, against the transforming influences of faith. It is one of the principal tasks of evangelization to lead those being evangelized to the sort of life which, in all its aspects, is ever more perfectly guided by the principles of faith.

5. *It is rooted in the community of faith.* God's plan of salvation supposes the community of faith; it creates that community and even actualizes and consummates itself within it. God calls us to himself within the community of faith, and within it and together with it we grow in faith.

A mature Christian must be willing to contribute generously to the realization of this community. This means that in his life of faith he accepts the help of the community with humility and gratitude, and that he contributes by personal dedication to the growth of faith within the community. The more someone matures, the more he will try to give more than he receives, but without imposing the norms of his contribution upon the community. Mature faith lets us serve without imposing ourselves; it allows us to accept without shame and to integrate ourselves without losing our own identity.

Before the Council, catechetics usually did not stress adequately the social dimension of faith. Under the influence of Vatican II, the General Catechetical Directory calls special attention to this dimension of faith, and also a genuine catechesis. This comes out even in its definition of catechesis: "Catechesis is that form of ecclesial action which leads both communities and individual members of the faithful to maturity of faith" (no. 21).

The Problem of Popular Faith and Religion

Catechesis evangelizes in the very measure that it leads those to be catechized to an ever more mature faith. In leading others to mature faith one often finds oneself confronted with a rather immature popular faith and religion. Thus we must get down to the delicate question about the place that is due to popular faith and religion in the process of faith maturation. But before we can deal meaningfully with this problem we must first clarify our notion of popular religion. It can mean quite different things.

Popular religion sometimes means simply an expression of religion that takes into account the capacity and true religious needs of ordinary people without higher education or special religious formation. The Gospel of salvation has been destined by God from its beginnings to be a Gospel to be preached to the poor, that is, the ordinary people. Christ himself in his evangelization gave us the example of preference for this social class.

Evangelization which addresses itself to people of this type must excel by its concrete and popular presentation, by the simplicity of its message and by its practical application to daily life. In addition it must fulfill the emotional aspects of religion.

Yet religion which corresponds in this way to the psychological and cultural condition of ordinary people can, at the same time, be outstanding for its depth and religious maturity. History provides us with splendid examples from all centuries of the Christian era. For this we have only to think of the primitive Christian community or of the Franciscan movement in the thirteenth century, or of the marvelous cases of a faith equally deep and simple that we encounter frequently in our own time. Only "poor" evangelists would be unaware that such people, although poor and uneducated, can be truly great in the Kingdom of God.

Popular religion in another positive sense can mean the necessary "incarnation" of religion in a respective culture. God never invites man in the abstract—the *homo ut sic* of scholastic philosophy—to a communion of life and love with him. Only concrete man who is always the product of his history and his environment "deserves" and receives the loving invitation of God. And only as a concrete and conditioned man can he and must he answer God's invitation.

The understanding and acceptance of God's challenge are already conditioned by the situation in which man receives it. And they are also conditioned by the individuality of the man who is invited. That is even more the case when man responds to God.

Man's answer to God is expressed in his religion. Religious expression, therefore, must vary according to the individuality of each man and according to the historical experiences and cultural conditions of his community. Whoever, for example, admits typical traits of particular cultures in the experience and actualization of life—and who would want to deny these?—must expect that these traits will be manifested in the particular ways that an American or a Spaniard experiences and expresses his religion. And further there will be a great difference between the expressions of a Mexican American and an American of Irish descent.

All this is obvious and commonly admitted as long as one deals with the abstract principle. The difficulties start from the moment one tries to apply this excellent principle to pastoral activities in daily life. Suddenly we are confronted with a host of delicate problems so loaded with emotions that impartial consideration becomes difficult. Thus it may be best to look at the problem as it regards the individual.

The Gospel calls man to a new way of life. This new life cannot mean a breaking-away from his individuality. What is good for him is supposed to be deepened after his conversion and eventually to come to perfection. But there are many elements that need purification, and often drastic changes will be needed, since these elements contradict a truly Christian existence or make it unduly difficult.

All this depends on the circumstances of the particular person. Some must change more, some less. But if anybody thinks he has nothing to change or only very little, he is in great danger of Pharisaism. In the following chapter, we shall see that the conversion to which the Gospel calls us is an ongoing process; it has to continue until the end of life. What is ample at the beginning will not be sufficient at later stages of this continuing transformation.

Applying these principles to the evangelization of large communities or whole cultures, we meet with another notion of popular religion. Here the phrase means the concrete way in which religion is expressed in a particular culture or ethnic group. In the last Synod of Bishops, popular religion, especially in relation to evangelization, was discussed. Bishop Eduardo Pironio of Mar del Plata, Argentina, presented a sympathetic description of popular religion, emphasizing its positive values but not denying its need for further purification (Report of October 10, 1974).

What interests us here is only the place of popular religion in a healthy life of faith and in the work of evangelization. For this, we submit the following principles.

1. Popular religion must be considered and accepted as the starting point for a new and deeper evangelization. We find valid and solid elements of authentic faith in it (Pironio Report). Any type of evangelization that disregards popular religion is unreal and violates a basic principle of authentic evangelization. Such an attitude is inexcusable in our times when we are stressing incessantly the norm that evangelization of non-Christians must take into account their religious heritage. Does this sound principle apply only to non-Christians and not to our brothers and sisters in Christ?

2. Popular religion, as we find it in Latin America and elsewhere, cannot, however, be taken as the point to be reached. It needs purification and interiorization and it must be related more effectively to daily life (Pironio Report).

3. In this process of purification, there is need for great patience and prudence and at the same time for dynamic firmness. It is simply unreal to demand, after so many years of neglect of this problem, that people now change radically overnight. The present situation would be much less difficult and delicate if the responsible leaders had not for so long supported their faithful in this kind of popular religion, which, as we now admit, is "impure" and imperfect.

The problem cannot be solved except by a uniform attitude and policy on the part of the clergy. Pastoral patience, indispensable in this effort, must not be confused with pastoral lassitude, which in theory admits the necessity of purification, but in fact defers it, sometimes for material motives.

4. Efforts made to achieve this necessary purification and interiorization must employ a positive approach. We should never start with negative criticism, but rather with sincere acknowledgement of positive values. Nothing should be taken away without first substituting something better. Above all, we must work for a new and deeper understanding of the core of the Christian message. This by itself will lead gradually to a more correct evaluation of what are the secondary elements that have

until now often received undue attention.

5. All this can best be done by leading people to a true appreciation and intensive use of the principal sources of authentic Christian spirituality—Scripture and liturgy.

We should, of course, never speak of the Blessed Mother without true respect, for we honor and love her. We should speak especially of her position in Scripture and the liturgy and of the way in which she is depicted there. Certainly, we should never approach her in a mere devotional sense. We should also speak much more of God, our heavenly Father, than of the Blessed Virgin and never give the impression that they are in any way on the same level as the father and mother within a family.

We must also insist on the central position due to the Holy Spirit in Christian religion and speak more of him than of St. Joseph or other saints, much as we truly love and honor them as members of our great heavenly brotherhood.

In the same vein, the Bible must be given a more prominent position than the rosary, and the basic Christian virtues of faith, love and justice must be accorded greater emphasis than any popular devotions. In addition, in dealing with popular devotions, we should always explain clearly how they have their roots in the fundamentals of Christian faith and how this relationship to the center of our faith gives them a place in our Christian religion.

Finally, we should never forget that what we call popular religion is often a style of religion that was quite apt and fitting in yesterday's world. But let us waste no time with useless criticism of past situations and practices. Rather, let us do everything we can to find the right expressions of true Christian faith for the men and women of today.

Chapter Three
Conversion:
The Other Aspect of Faith

When we make a commitment of faith, we accept the invitation of God who calls us to a new life in union with him. This new life demands a profound change in our existence, and this change is what we call conversion. Our "yes" of faith would be a lie if it did not include the change of attitude and action that God expects from his sons and friends.

Thus conversion is only another aspect of our commitment of faith and the change which comes about in our lives is the best proof of the sincerity of our commitment. If we understand evangelization as it was explained by the Fourth Synod of Bishops, i.e., as "the activity whereby the Church proclaims the Gospel so that the faith may be aroused, may unfold and may grow" (The Evangelization of the Modern World, p. 12), evangelization must by its nature lead to conversion.

Conversion—The Main Request of Evangelization

The place due to conversion in genuine evangelization is clearly expressed in the preaching of Christ himself. At the beginning of his Gospel, St. Mark sums up in one single verse the quintessence of Christ's evangelization. "The time has come," Jesus said, "and the Kingdom of God is close at hand. Repent, and believe the Good News" (Mk. 1:15).

Jesus congratulates his listeners because they live in the messianic age, the time eagerly awaited for so long. They have a unique opportunity, but all depends upon one indispensable con-

dition: they must repent, must change their lives. Christ characterizes his entire preaching as a call to repentance: "I have not
come to call the virtuous but sinners to repentance" (Lk. 5:32).
All those who consider themselves righteous and think they
have no need of repentance exclude themselves from the bless-
ings of salvation.

When, on the day of Pentecost, the evangelization of the
Church began, the sermon of Peter culminates in a call to a
change of life: "You must repent and every one of you must be
baptized in the name of Jesus Christ for the forgiveness of your
sins, and you will receive the gift of the Holy Spirit" (Acts
2:38). Without this change, baptism would not save them.

St. Paul, at the end of an apostolic life so dedicated to the
proclamation of the Gospel, summarizes his whole work as a
continuous invitation to repentance: "I could not disobey the
heavenly vision. On the contrary I started preaching, first to the
people of Damascus, then to those in Jerusalem and all the
countryside of Judea, and also to the pagans, urging them to
repent and to turn to God, proving their change of heart by
their deeds" (Acts 26:19f).

In the light of these biblical texts we can readily understand
the emphasis that the General Catechetical Directory puts on
the role of conversion in the whole of catechetical activity. In
any final analysis, it is its identity with faith that justifies for
conversion its central position in catechesis. "The element of
conversion is always present in the dynamism of faith" (no. 18).
"Faith is a gift of God which calls men to conversion" (no. 22).
Catechists should never forget that "the act of faith necessarily
involves a conversion of the one making it" (no. 75).

The same emphasis on conversion is also found in the preparatory text of the Synod of Bishops: "Since faith is the basis
of the whole Christian life, it is necessary that everything done
in the Church (preaching, theological research, organization,
worship, institutions, etc.) should be directed toward ensuring
that individuals and communities become converted to God,
who communicates himself to us in Christ, and that they should
progress and live in this conversion" (p. 14).

Before the kerygmatic renewal of the 1950s, catechesis did

not insist very much upon conversion. The new emphasis resulted mainly from the diligent study of the New Testament and, as a result of these biblical studies, a deeper understanding of divine revelation and faith.

It had always been stressed that the main objective of catechesis was leading those being catechized to faith, but, as we have seen, faith then was understood, above all, as intellectual assent to the truths revealed by God. However, such faith does not yet include conversion; at best, it disposes for conversion.

On the other hand, faith as we have described it in the last chapter according to Scripture and Vatican II consists precisely in the acceptance of God's call and in a determined commitment to a new life. In such a case evangelization obviously challenges us to authentic conversion, and such conversion is precisely the aim of evangelization.

In religious education overemphasis on the intellectual element of faith does little to foster true conversion; in fact, it can render conversion more difficult. Yet at the same time we must insist that neglecting the intellectual aspect of faith can also have harmful consequences, since it can lead to an emotional faith lacking in depth. Such faith relies more on vague and transitory feelings than on the solid motives demanded in a mature commitment.

Any careful reflection on the meaning and place of evangelization in God's plan of salvation shows us immediately that evangelization calls for faith and, together with faith, for a true change in our life-style. But in what sense can we call such change a real "conversion"? And what does this conversion really imply in our lives? We will answer these questions in the next section.

What Does Authentic Conversion Mean?

In the most common acceptance of the word, "conversion" means a radical change to a better life by someone who hitherto has lived a bad life. In this sense we speak of the conversion of a great sinner.

It is obvious that in our case we do not wish to imply that evangelization concerns itself only with great sinners who need drastic changes in their lives. Nevertheless, we insist that evangelization aims at a "conversion" in the strict sense, according to the etymological meaning of the word. We really mean a turning-around to a better way of life.

True, the starting point in such a conversion is not necessarily a bad or undisciplined life, but it has to be at least a still unsatisfactory life that needs to be changed into a more mature and fulfilled one. And this change means precisely a "con-version," that is, a reorientation of the converted person who turns toward God as the goal and meaning of his entire human life.

It is worthwhile to examine somewhat more thoroughly the starting point for this change of life and also the point to be reached. As already mentioned, we do not always find the starting point to be a deliberate opposition to God or to what is considered good. Often, it is just a more or less noticeable absence of God in planning one's life and living it from day to day.

Before his conversion, a man is not sufficiently aware of the meaning of his life. He lives it thoughtlessly without realizing that a selfish attitude influences his various activities. In any case, the starting point for conversion is a life that is not yet entirely oriented toward God.

Let us take as an example the rather exceptional case of a child with a good natural disposition who grows up in an excellent Christian family. He is cut out to be a model Christian. Even in this most favorable and therefore rare case, our little child must convert himself from a kind of life where, though naturally good, he is still immature to the still more perfect service of God that results from a mature commitment of faith and love. Even this exemplary child must change for the better as he grows and matures. However, he will, of course, experience his conversion in a very different way than St. Paul or St. Augustine.

The profound change which is characteristic of any genuine conversion can be considered in two ways. On the one hand, it means a break with the past; on the other, it means a further growth of the good already present in the convert before his conversion, although it might not have been in the foreground.

Some people have to change more than others, and some will change more rapidly than others. The more someone has to change and the more rapidly he changes, the more he will experience his conversion as a break with the past. Conversely, the less one's previous attitudes and actions have gone directly against God, the more he will experience his conversion as an organic and continuous development of his personality without any real break with the past.

In a normal conversion, we encounter both aspects, that of break and that of growth. A solid evangelization must take account of both dimensions according to the particular situation of the convert. In former times, we often put too much emphasis upon the break with the past and insisted too strongly upon the violent character of this break. Today we are more in danger of minimizing the necessary element of break.

We have already insisted that the correct solution demands a balance of both aspects. Scripture certainly does not favor the elimination of the break aspect. The ineffable mercy of the Father is offered to the prodigal son who breaks with his shameful past. However, there is no line in Scripture that says all sinners resemble the prodigal son to the same degree. Man in the Middle Ages liked to exaggerate his sinfulness; modern man needs to be reminded of his sinfulness, but we must be aware that he is sensitive to exaggeration.

We must also keep in mind that the conversion of even the worst sinner must involve some continuity with his past life. Without this continuity, conversion would result in schizophrenia. How much of their past experiences and characteristic attitudes were retained by such great converts as St. Paul, St. Augustine and St. Ignatius Loyola!

We best convey to modern man the value of break with the past when we present it as a liberation from his own selfishness, without any doubt difficult and painful but at the same time leading to a great and joyful experience of life. Such liberation is, in fact, the deep theological meaning of any true conversion. What separates us from God is ultimately always our own selfishness.

Conversion consists in the gradual liberation of man from all selfishness and the total dedication of the liberated "ego" to God. The dedication of an ego that is not yet liberated is a lie or, at least, a great self-deception.

In the light of this explanation, the point to be reached in conversion also becomes clear. Conversion, by its essence, means something more than the correction of some particular defects. What needs changing, above all, is the hitherto insufficient orientation of one's whole life toward God as the Lord, our meaning and fulfillment. God alone deserves man's total love, and this love without reserve actualizes itself in a total surrender to God. The more a conversion results from such loving surrender, the more it is a perfect conversion.

In order to avoid all possible misunderstanding, it may be wise to mention that we are not here dealing with the value of merely implicit faith in the process of salvation. We do not deny in any way that all those can attain salvation who are searching for God, at least, implicitly, "and, moved by God's grace, strive by their deeds to do his will as it is known to them through the dictates of conscience" (*Constitution on the Church*, no. 16).

But here we are dealing with the faith to which evangelization has to lead. This faith is explicit and requires a conscious conversion to God as the only one who can claim our total submission and deserves all our service and love. A merely "horizontal" spirituality which concerns itself only with the integration of man into his environment and does not consciously ascend to God can never satisfy the indispensable demands of a true conversion.

With this clarification, we also wish to make clear the personal character of such a conversion. What counts, more than anything else, is a new personal attitude toward God whom we accept as the absolute Lord and, at the same time, as the loving Father. If this acceptance of God is sincere and not just lip service, it must have profound consequences on the whole of one's life.

The decisive difference between a superficial and a "radical" conversion in the strict meaning of the word consists precisely in this: a radical conversion demands a change at the root, the Latin word for root being "radix" from which the word "radical" comes. It changes the very root of one's particular acts, that is, the basic attitude which determines the transcendental orientation of our actions and confers upon them their religious and moral values.

In a superficial conversion only the exterior actions are being changed without any deep reorientation of the nucleus of the responsible person. Surely God prefers a repentant sinner, who, in spite of his sincere conversion, still out of weakness lapses at times into his former sins, to a self-righteous man who without any noticeable exterior vice lives for himself alone without any personal relationship to God. The interior element of true conversion is very clearly expressed in the Greek word for conversion, "metanoia," by which Scripture describes the change (meta) of the heart (noe). The change of our actions counts in the measure that they are rooted in the change of our minds and hearts.

Since man so easily deceives himself and often confuses mere feelings with a true commitment, Scripture rightly emphasizes the "works" by which man must prove the interior change: "If you are repentant, produce the appropriate fruits" (Lk. 3:8; see also Acts 26:19f).

In the past we sometimes spoke too often about the works of repentance and did not speak enough of the work of conversion. What I want to say is this: after sin, the sinner must repent. Sincere and deep repentance has the natural tendency to actualize itself by works of repentance. Today when we are in danger of minimizing sin, we are also in danger of minimizing the works of repentance. If penitential practices are done in the spirit of true Christian repentance and therefore with a new love after the forgiveness of sin, they can greatly help the repentant Christian in his journey to God. In this sense Scripture supposes and often recommends works of repentance.

But when the Bible insists upon the change of heart (metanoia), it requires much more than just penitential practices. It demands, above all, a new way of life governed by an unconditional acceptance of the Gospel. And this must involve all of the spheres of one's life, gradually leading to a reform of one's entire existence in the spirit of the Gospel.

In his great love God gives us time to make this change gradually. Without a miracle it cannot be achieved at one given moment. What we usually call a conversion is only the marked beginning of a profound interior and exterior change which according to God's plan has to continue and to deepen through life until it is consummated in a Christian death.

And, of course, such a change cannot continue indefinitely with the joy and excitement of its first moments. Regardless, the effort must go on in an ever more effective reorientation of one's whole existence. We are faced here with another important aspect of genuine evangelization: it not only invites us to that initial conversion but must also go on and foster a gradual transformation of the convert into a new man in accordance with God's will, leading him to the maturity of Christ (Eph. 4:13; Rom. 8:29).

We should definitely expect a catechist who is evangelizing to stimulate such conversion not only by his teaching but even more by his personal witness. He must distinguish himself by the generous efforts he is making in his own life. That the catechist is not yet a perfect Christian, everyone must understand, for this is simply a part of the human condition.

God does not chose to evangelize us through angels but through converted brothers and sisters who have to walk with us in the same journey of ongoing purification. But if the catechist himself is not striving to become a model Christian, he loses his credibility and his evangelizing power. "Hypocrite," the Lord would tell him, "first take the plank out of your own eye and then you will be able to see clearly enough to take the splinter out of your brother's eye" (Mt. 7:5).

As we have seen, evangelizing catechesis calls all men and not only notorious sinners to a profound change of life. Furthermore, its call for conversion is addressed not only to individuals but also to the entire Christian community. In the past we usually did not place enough emphasis on this social dimension of conversion. We always admitted the necessity for individual conversion but we were inclined to overlook the need of the Christian community for a continual conversion.

Ever since the Protestant Reformation, Catholics have been overly eager to exalt the ecclesial community and to defend everything that the community, as such, did and thought. It took Vatican II to end this erroneous attitude. The pilgrim Church in its totality will always remain essentially imperfect, and therefore it will always be in need of continuous and profound reform (Ecclesia semper reformanda).

Just as catechesis given by individuals loses its credibility as soon as the catechist ceases to strive for personal conversion, so too the Christian community loses its credibility as transmitter of the Gospel if it does not humbly admit its obvious defects and strive vigorously to achieve necessary reforms. In the preparation for the last Synod of Bishops, this theme was formulated graphically in the passage on conversion: conversion or metanoia, the main objective of evangelization, is a condition and a permanent obligation of the pilgrim Church.

A valid objection to the last Synod, it seems to us, consists in the observation that the theme of conversion, and with it the theme of the reform of the Christian community, did not receive adequate emphasis. Does this mean that even responsible leaders still do not fully comprehend the urgency of a profound conversion that is both individual and corporate?

Most people will admit that the institutional Church has, in fact, lost much of its credibility. This was mentioned often and clearly in the reports of the Synod. A Church that does not make itself credible evangelizes in vain. This credibility must be restored, especially in the local communities, because it is there that the Church can be seen by everyone and makes the greatest impression.

When the General Catechetical Directory (no. 21) says that all catechetical activity consists in leading both the community and individual Christians to an ever more mature faith, this must surely mean that authentic catechesis must lead individuals and community to a genuine conversion.

Chapter Four
Pre-Evangelization

Since making a thorough analysis of missionary catechetics some twenty years ago, leaders in this field have insisted time and again that an initial and fundamental catechesis must precede a more detailed presentation of the individual mysteries of Christian faith. This proclamation of the Gospel, these leaders assert, must concentrate on the core of the Christian message, which they with St. Paul call "kerygma." In addition, it must lead to a first commitment to Christ as Lord and Savior.

But in addition to this step, it is also being stressed that under ordinary circumstances the first proclamation of the Gospel should be preceded by a preliminary stage commonly known as pre-catechesis. This serves to prepare the candidate gradually for the first proclamation, which then with God's grace will lead to the initial commitment.

Considering the fact that the vast majority of those to be evangelized for the first time need such pre-evangelization, the silence of the last Synod of Bishops about this step is somewhat surprising. Of the official texts of the Synod, only the preliminary text mentions pre-evangelization in passing, and that only in connection with the function of the mass media in the work of evangelization.

The silence of the Synod can be understood in part by its intention to deal with evangelization itself. Moreover it can be said that in the Synod's significant acceptance of evangelization in the broader sense, pre-evangelization is, in fact, included as the more remote preparation for the first commitment of faith. Indeed, if evangelization is understood as the activity whereby the Church proclaims the Gospel so that faith may be aroused, pre-evangelization is surely the first step of this proclamation.

Yet, it may also be that the overemphasis on pre-evangelization, as we find it in some of the catechetical literature in recent years, contributed to the silence of the Synod. One exaggeration, however, ought not to be counteracted by an exaggeration in the opposite sense. In any case it cannot be denied that pre-evangelization has an important role in the whole process of evangelization.

When Is Pre-Evangelization Needed?

There are cases where non-Christians without any preparation by those who act as catechists find themselves sufficiently disposed to accept at once the message of salvation. Through a favorable combination of events in their lives and under the influence of a special grace, they are already prepared for God's call. No more is needed than to present to them explicitly the good tidings of God's love.

But such cases, as every missionary knows, are exceptions. Generally, it is a long and tedious process that leads from someone's first interest in the Christian religion to the initial commitment of faith. It is a process that normally needs years. First encounters with Christianity—for example, the occasion of an unfavorable presentation through mass media or of partial information learned from an acquaintance—often result in negative attitudes toward this foreign religion from the West which is strange and not to be taken seriously.

In such cases where a negative image already exists, the first show of positive interest is vital and does not normally happen suddenly. Moreover, this first appreciation does not imply any intention to become a Christian. At best, it implies a desire to know a bit more about the Christian way of living and thinking. Perhaps, also, there is a readiness to enter into a friendly dialogue, a willingness to learn and to acknowledge the value of the other side.

That is all that can be expected for the moment. Such a positive attitude is still very far from the first serious thoughts of conversion, and such first thoughts of conversion are even farther from an initial commitment of explicit faith. But it is precisely by this initial commitment that the candidate is able to open himself to initiation in the Christian mysteries in a spirit of faith. Who can deny that missionary activity in the strict sense consists especially in the loving service offered during this long, often difficult journey from initial attraction to the first commitment of faith?

The special difficulties of missionary work are encountered particularly in this early stage. Mistakes committed here cannot easily be rectified in the later stages of religious formation; often they may never be straightened out. It is for this reason that missionary catechetics in the past twenty years has dealt so carefully with the problem of pre-evangelization.

But pre-evangelization is not a problem only for missionary catechesis. We meet it with the same urgency in the evangelization of baptized persons who have never fully committed themselves to a Christian life as well as in the conversion of faithful who have lost their faith and their living contact with the Church. True, the difficulties in these cases are of a different type from those encountered in missionary activity, but in the final analysis we encounter the same basic problem—the problem of a gradual preparation for a willing acceptance of the Gospel.

Many adolescents today are also presenting a special problem. After a Christian education in childhood, they have lost interest in their religion and often resent it profoundly. These young people are not helped—in fact, they may be further alienated—by a systematic explanation of the mysteries of Christian faith.

What they need, above all, is much more basic help toward a new appreciation of the faith and a new religious outlook on life. Without this reorientation of their lives, the particular mysteries of faith will mean nothing to them. But such reorientation supposes a new and solid evangelization, and such evangelization cannot be effective without some form of pre-evangelization.

Hitherto, we considered pre-evangelization to be a separate stage of catechetical activity that preceded evangelization and prepared for it. But there is also a kind of pre-evangelization that may aptly be described as "concurrent." Its necessity and special function become obvious with reflection on the pastoral situation which today characterizes much of the Christian world.

Many Christians who still regularly practice their religion and sincerely describe themselves as faithful are not aware that, under the influence of the mass media, they have, in fact, accepted many un-Christian principles and attitudes. To be sure, they do not deny the Blessed Mother. Yet their religion forms an enclave neatly separated from the other spheres of their existence. In these spheres, they evaluate and live according to un-Christian principles. (See the pertinent description of this pastoral situation in the General Catechetical Directory, no. 5.)

Despite such illogical ways of thinking, these Christians believe they are living a Christian life. Their faith, however, lacks a solid foundation and is, therefore, in danger; it could probably not survive an acute crisis. But it is possible and even quite probable that they themselves, because of their generally conservative attitudes, will never stop practicing their religion. Their children, on the other hand, more exposed to the destructive influence of these un-Christian principles, lack such conservative inhibitions, and, as a consequence, will abandon their religion.

In the modern pastoral situation, concurrent pre-evangelization must fill an important function of providing a necessary rational foundation for faith. The term "concurrent pre-evangelization" may seem a misnomer. It does, however, indicate a logical priority in relationship to evangelization if not a temporal priority. Concurrent pre-evangelization is an activity simultaneous with evangelization, but by way of logical priority it provides the necessary foundation for evangelization.

What Are the Particular Objectives
of Pre-Evangelization?

From what we have indicated in the preceding section, it

should be clear that the basic objective of pre-evangelization consists in preparing the unbeliever for the first presentation of the Gospel. Whenever someone is still unable to accept the message of salvation in faith, he needs pre-evangelization to bring him to the proper disposition. We have also seen in the last section that pre-evangelization can encompass everything from the first vague interest up to the threshold of faith. Now we may ask what pre-evangelization does to help someone along this long and rather difficult journey.

The more important objectives of pre-evangelization may be dealt with most effectively through their temporal sequence. The whole process of preparation for faith begins with the awakening of interest in Christianity, its doctrines and especially its way of life. In response, appropriate information should be offered with prudence and truthfulness. The more a candidate's interest grows, the more apt pre-evangelization will stimulate him in his search for truth.

In doing so, however, he will almost necessarily encounter obstacles that will hinder his progress toward full truth and its relation to his own life. Pre-evangelization has to assist him in overcoming these difficulties, while at the same time it is leading him to the initial conviction that the Christian religion is true and appropriate for him.

We do not want to say that these different aspects can always be clearly distinguished in each particular case. In missionary catechesis, we can usually distinguish them clearly as different stages of the whole process, whereas in concurrent pre-evangelization we may encounter only some of these elements and without any fixed sequence. But it is always worthwhile to distinguish them methodically in order to better understand the function and dynamics of pre-evangelization.

Much of the effectiveness of pre-evangelization is determined by the way in which initial information, given to awaken interest in Christianity, is imparted. Information obtrusively given invariably repels more than it attracts. Instruction must always be succinct, impartial, exact and at the same time well adapted to the particular situations of those to whom it is addressed.

Personal contact, whenever possible, should be used to deepen and individualize information provided through printed materials such as brochures. Accurate, well-presented materials are without doubt enormous helps in forming Christians who are able to live their faith in all its fullness and beauty, but even more important is the faith witness of Christians already committed and of their communities. The missionary charism to a great extent involves the ability to develop under the influence of grace the seeds sown in initial personal encounters with Christian existence.

A true conversion can come about in very different ways. In all of them, however, the candidate will come into an ever more personal contact with God while at the same time his initial interest is being deepened and purified. The initial interest results not infrequently from motives that need further purification before they can substantiate a solid conversion. It is precisely the task of pre-evangelization to assist with prudence, discretion and zeal in this process of purifying motives and deepening insights and convictions.

On his way to God, the convert meets many obstacles. How few conversions take place without any serious difficulty! The task of pre-evangelization does not so much consist in eliminating them as in the help it offers in overcoming them.

The major problems in conversion are almost never of a mere intellectual nature, and thus they cannot be overcome simply by responding to the intellectual aspects of the problem. Yet, intellectual difficulties must also be taken seriously. In the pre-evangelization of educated people, the catechist should guard especially against giving quick, ready-made answers.

Such a response may easily give the impression that the difficulty is not being taken seriously. Instead, the catechist should indicate that he appreciates the weight of the problem and wants to reply to it. The more educated and intelligent the prospective convert, the more we help him by merely pointing out the elements of a satisfactory solution, leaving him to the task of drawing conclusions and accepting them as his own.

Today we meet countless Christians who do not experience or recognize the presence of God in their lives. They do not deny his existence; he just does not exist for them. They live in an "absence of God" which affects and characterizes their whole lives.

In company with Vatican II the General Catechetical Directory calls special attention to this absence of God as one of the most outstanding characteristics of today's religious situation (no. 5). Christians who suffer in this way from God's absence receive very little help if presented only with the scholastic proofs for the existence of God. What they need is to discover him present and active in their own lives and the only one who can give full meaning to their existence.

These marginal Christians, whose ranks include many young people, really need a basic pre-evangelization before they can ever wholeheartedly accept the message of salvation. In dealing with them, we must remember that their main difficulty often results from a distorted image of God and consequently of life. Any new idea of God presented must not only accord with a world profoundly affected by modern scientific advances but must also give a unity and clarity to that world far beyond what science alone can achieve.

In the notion of God handed down to us by our ancestors, he also functioned as a substitute for man's inability to master the blind and mysterious powers of the universe. Even today man still encounters countless situations which he cannot plan or master or even predict. Thanks to medical science, he can prolong his life and protect it from many dangers. Yet in old age he cannot start his life over again or prolong it indefinitely. Only utopian thinkers look for a future in which man will be sovereign over all situations.

However, the increase in man's powers has been such that he is increasingly uninterested in a God who seems superfluous, a refuge in desperate but rare crises. For this man a new image of God must be presented—as one who transcends the entire world including man now and in the future. But this thoroughly transcendent God must, at the same time, be experienced and understood as an entirely immanent God who lives and reigns within his world, a God who is the very root and deepest reason for all that concerns man and his universe.

An authentic image is, of course, important not only for Christians who have lost confidence in the traditional picture of God. It would be foolish and inexcusable not to give a modern image of God in both pre-evangelization and evangelization alike. The effect of modern progress upon man's attitudes is perhaps the most decisive reason why so-called popular religion must be purified of the old image of God that it preserves with such remarkable tenacity. The consequences can only be disastrous in a world that is changing so rapidly and profoundly.

Merely clearing away obstacles blocking a path does not bring one any closer to one's goal. On the way to God, much more must be done than just clearing away obstacles to faith. Faith itself must be fostered from the very beginning. Even a positive presentation of the reasons for a commitment of faith is not enough. True personal contact with God is needed, and that starts and deepens only in an atmosphere of prayer.

What Type of Approach Characterizes Authentic Pre-Evangelization?

The right approach is of great importance in all catechetical activity but especially so in pre-evangelization. Here the catechist enagages in the delicate task of influencing people who are still indifferent or even opposed or frightened by a commitment of faith that will so thoroughly change their lives. The approach in pre-evangelization must therefore be marked by the following qualities.

The most fundamental is a deep and loving understanding of the unbeliever and of his human and religious situation. Without such amicable acceptance, true dialogue is impossible. If ever it was possible to convert people by authoritarian monologues from above, that time is surely past, and we have no regrets that it is.

In pre-evangelization, we also need a real understanding of the indifference and even of the atheism of today's unbeliever. Here we can learn much from Vatican II. It is obvious that the Church, today, as always, rejects any form of atheism; "still, she strives to detect the hidden causes for the denial of God. Conscious of how weighty are the questions which atheism raises and motivated by love for all men, she believes these questions ought to be examined seriously and more profoundly" (*Constitution on the Church in the Modern World*, no. 21).

Obviously, it is not enough to ponder or to understand the reasons for modern indifferentism and atheism; what is even more necessary is an understanding of the individual person who is suffering from these conditions. As a consequence there must be an adaptation of the Christian message for each person, one which keeps in mind his particular needs and problems.

The catechist must accept each candidate as an individual in a particular life situation. The end goal is the same for all who received pre-evangelization, but the starting point will probably differ in each case. The "art" and "secret" of superior pre-evangelization consists especially in this ability to adapt.

Patience is also necessary. Modern man does not like to be pushed; if we fail to give him the necessary time for his own inquiry and decision, he will probably not give us his confidence. In the past, missionary activity was not infrequently characterized by a kind of impatience. In a way this can be understood if we consider the former, erroneous supposition that only those who professed the Catholic faith could be saved. Their apostolic zeal tended to make those missionaries of yesterday somewhat impatient, although without objective reason. Today, the Council assures us that those who seek God are already walking in the way of salvation (*Constitution on the Church*, no. 16).

On the other hand, the impatience of some missionaries in the past does not justify any modern excess in the opposite direction. As in any journey, so in the journey of faith, undue loss of time diminishes vigor. If such loss is not just the result of indecision or tardiness on the part of the catechist, but stems from some lack of true religious zeal, then it would mean a serious defect.

Chapter Five
Our Gospel

Irrigation projects are planned and built to provide fields with water; evangelization is planned and carried out to provide man with the Gospel, that is, the message of salvation. True, evangelization may not confine itself simply to the proclamation of the Gospel; it is not enough for man to listen to it. We must help him to accept it with his whole heart and to live it with dedication and perseverance.

The whole work of evangelization, nevertheless, is concerned with the adequate transmission of an important message for man. And this, immediately, confronts us with a serious problem: Are we not in danger of overstressing the message by seeing it in this way. Christianity is above all a new way of experiencing and living God's presence! In order to answer this problem, we must take account of the peculiarity of the Christian message.

The Nature of the Gospel We Proclaim

Pre-conciliar theology and catechesis commonly considered divine revelation as the totality of truths revealed by God. God revealed these truths so that man, in view of God's authority, would accept them. In this view, evangelization means above all the transmission of truths in order that man by his submission will acknowledge God as his Lord.

Vatican II was eager to correct this way of looking at divine revelation. In its most basic document, the *Constitution on Divine Revelation*, the Council characterized revelation clearly as a personal communication of God with man, by which God intends primarily a union of love and life: "In his goodness and wisdom, God chose to reveal himself and to make known to us the hidden purpose of his will (cf. Eph. 2:18; 2 Pet. 1:4). Through this revelation, therefore, the invisible God (cf. Col. 1:15; 1 Tim. 1:17) out of the abundance of his love speaks to man as friends (cf. Ex. 33:11; Jn. 15:14-15) and lives among them (cf. Bar. 3:38) so that he may invite and take them into fellowship with himself" (n. 2).

In other words, since God loves us, he invites to a deep and lasting friendship with himself. In this, the Council's view, the main task of all those who transmit divine revelation is not the transmission of a set of truths. Their principal task is to lead man to a true friendship with God and to let him grow in it.

This, of course, does not deny that the catechist has to communicate truths of great importance; it only means that the principal aim of his work consists in leading man to a union of love with God and that communication of particular doctrines must be seen in the light of man's friendship with God which is the goal of God's speaking to man.

The following comparison may help us to realize the great difference between the pre-conciliar and the conciliar understanding of revelation and evangelization. After his lecture at the university, Professor Smith calls his friend Jim and invites him to spend his next vacation with him in Italy. Both in his lecture and in his phone call, the professor transmits a message. In the lecture, however, his special aim is the scholarly transmission of a complex set of theoretical truths which constitute the subject matter of his teaching. His students take pains to understand and assimilate them. If Professor Smith teaches well and approaches his students with a friendly attitude, his efforts will lead to good personal relationships with his students. But this is a by-product of his teaching and not its principal aim.

When the professor invites his friend Jim to Italy, however, we see a personal communication. He wishes primarily to express his friendship with Jim and to stimulate him to accept the invitation. In such a case, the main aim of the message is not communicational knowledge but the fostering of their mutual friendship. In order to make this a reality, the invitation by phone is needed, but what matters most is not the message as such but the camaraderie with Jim during the vacation in Italy.

We find exactly the same thing in the case of our Gospel message. God speaks to us as friends and invites us to a great and joyful union with him forever. The message proclaimed is not an end in itself, but the necessary means to accomplish God's plan of salvation by leading man to a union of life and love with him. As the Council insists in the text we just quoted, God manifests himself to us because he loves us. This opening of himself to man is in itself a manifestation of his tremendous love.

God can manifest himself without an intermediary, but, in fact, he chose to manifest himself through intermediaries: "At various times in the past and in various ways, God spoke to our ancestors through the prophets; but in our own time, in the last days, he has spoken to us through his Son" (Heb. 1:1f).

Today Christ continues his prophetic office through the evangelizing catechesis of the Church. All its evangelization proclaims God's loving plan of salvation. What finally counts in this evangelization, of course, is not the message as such but the new life to which it invites and leads.

Nevertheless, evangelization must concern itself directly with the message just as efficient irrigation must concern itself directly with the distribution of water and not with the harvest. Yet, obviously, what counts in the end is not the water but the harvest which alone justifies the hard and costly work of irrigation. If irrigation does not provide water, it provides nothing. It is useless to hope for a wonderful harvest in a desert where there is no water available.

The comparison with irrigation helps us to understand another aspect of the Gospel and its transmission through evangelization. Irrigation does not produce water; it only distributes it efficiently. It must bring water to all segments of the farmland without losing water on the way and without deteriorating or poisoning it. Irrigation always supposes a source of water that feeds it.

In the same way evangelization does not produce the Gospel but transmits it. The "evangelist" does not beget the Gospel message; it is not the product of his own speculation or religious experience. Rather, he receives the message from God who alone is the author of the Gospel. We should keep ourselves aware that the Gospel we proclaim is also not a product of the Church.

The Church, however, has received the Gospel, and under the guidance of the Holy Spirit, it must preserve, develop and transmit that Gospel. By accepting the Gospel from the Church, we have the necessary guarantee that we basically understand it in the right way. We should never forget that, in our work of evangelization, we act in the service of God but are authorized and guided by the Church.

As the message of God's love, the Gospel is by its nature good news. Since God loves us, he speaks to us and invites us to share in his own life and existence. In his love, he wants to make our lives great, happy and fulfilled. This means that the Gospel is by its nature a message for man, since God has made him for final union with himself.

Adept evangelization thus has to convey and show in a striking manner the way that the Gospel answers the deepest and most genuine longings of man. This does not mean that the Gospel can be interpreted merely by philosophical reflection. God's invitation to us far surpasses philosophy's ability to interpret it. The Gospel promises something essentially more than man's total development of his human life.

Human development has an important place in the Gospel message as we shall see in a later chapter; here, however, we must stress the transcendence of the Gospel. "For God in his wisdom made it impossible for men to know him by means of their own wisdom. Instead God decided to save those who believe, by means of the 'foolish' message we preach . . . since what seems to be God's foolishness is stronger than men's wisdom and what seems to be God's weakness is stronger than man's strength" (1 Cor. 1:21-25). "The things that no eye has seen and no ear has heard, things beyond the mind of man, all that God has prepared for those who love him" (1 Cor. 2:9).

Because of its transcendence, the Gospel message requires special efforts in order to be correctly understood and transmitted. The Catholic Church, therefore, has from the beginning taken great care to transmit the Gospel without error. But it has not always been clearly seen that the correct transmission of the Gospel requires more than a correct presentation of the various doctrines. A comparison from life may help to illustrate what is required for correct transmission.

An agent is engaged to assist in the transfer of a beautiful home to a new owner. Before he delivers the house, however, the agent demolishes it and hands over to the owner "faithfully" all the stones and lumber and other material of the old construction. Would this not be a crime of faithlessness? Who would not want to send the agent to prison, or, better yet, to an asylum?

As this poor agent acted, so does a "faithful" messenger of the Gospel who correctly transmits the particular doctrines of faith but without clearly showing the main meaning and the inter-relationship of the whole message. If one does not become aware of the loving intention of God "to reveal himself and to make known to us the hidden purpose of his will" (*Constitution on Divine Revelation*, no. 2), knowledge of the particular doctrines will be of very little help.

God does not just desire by his revelation to provide us with a long list of unconnected truths; he wants to challenge us through this plan to a new life in union with him. Since in preconciliar catechesis this decisive point of authentic evangelization often did not receive due emphasis, the Council called very special attention to it in the paragraph quoted above.

In presenting this central point of the Christian message clearly, the faithful messenger must not permit details to divert him from the main content. He is, however, not allowed to neglect or, even worse, falsify the minor elements. He has received this message in order to transmit it in its entirety to his brothers and sisters, keeping in mind the particular needs and the disposition of each congregation.

Since the Christian message of salvation is so rich and also somewhat complex, it is necessary that all listeners be exposed to the main themes. Any who are capable and disposed to receive the message in its entirety should be given it. It is in this sense that the Council speaks of a "hierarchy of truths" in Christian revelation (*Decree on Ecumenism*, no. 11). The General Catechetical Directory explains what is really meant by this expression: "This hierarchy does not mean that some truths pertain to faith less than others, but rather that some truths are based on others as of higher priority and are illuminated by them. On all levels catechesis should take account of this hierarchy of the truths of faith" (no. 43).

The whole New Testament gives testimony to the fact that the preaching of the apostolic Church put great emphasis on one central message which dominated its whole evangelization: the manifestation of God's saving power and love through his Son, Jesus Christ. Among all the apostles, St. Paul most excels by his continuous emphasis on this core of the Christian message, which implicitly includes all the rest and which must be proclaimed to all who are to be evangelized.

St. Paul calls this core of the Christian message the "kerygma," that is, *the message*, in the meaning of the central and main message, that includes virtually all the rest. At other times he calls it *the mystery* and means the central mystery which is proclaimed by the apostles; it is the "mystery of Christ" or God's work of salvation that has Christ as its center: "You have probably heard how I have been entrusted by God with the grace he meant for you, and that it was by a revelation that I was given the knowledge of the mystery. . . . To me was given the grace to preach the depths that I see in the mystery of Christ and to explain how the mystery is to be dispensed and how comprehensive God's wisdom really is, according to the plan which he had from all eternity in Jesus Christ our Lord" (Eph. 3:2-11). With this we also have St. Paul's precise answer to the important question: What is, after all, the core of the Gospel that we have to proclaim to all men?

The Core of the Gospel

Owing to thorough studies on the message of the New Testament, as well as on the origin and the life of the primitive

Church, we have nowadays reached an imposing consensus about the key elements of evangelization in apostolic times. As all admit today, we encounter in the center of the apostolic preaching the forceful proclamation of an unheard-of event, the Christ event.

This event is so fundamental that with it a new era begins for man. It gives him a new opportunity for unlimited dimension; it gives new meaning to his life. In the light of this decisive event, the past must be considered as a preparation (cf. Heb. 1:1-3; Gal. 3:24): "Without any doubt, the mystery of our religion is very deep indeed; he was made visible in the flesh, attested by the Spirit, seen by angels, proclaimed by pagans, believed in the world, taken up in glory" (1 Tim. 3:16).

"When the appointed time came"—the "fullness of time" (cf. Eph. 1:10)—"God sent his Son, born of a woman, born a subject of the law, to redeem the subjects of the law and to enable us to be adopted as sons. The proof that you are sons is that God has sent the Spirit of his Son into our hearts, the Spirit that cries, 'Abba Father,' and it is this that makes you a son: You are not a slave anymore; and if God made you son, then he has made you heir" (Gal. 4:4-7).

"God is love. God's love for us was revealed when God sent into the world his only Son so that we could have life through him; this is the love I mean: not our love for God but God's love for us when he sent his Son to be the sacrifice that takes away our sins. My dear people, since God has loved us so much, we too should love one another" (1 Jn. 4:8-11).

"Think of the love that the Father has lavished on us by letting us be called God's children; and that is what we are. Because the world refused to acknowledge him, therefore it does not acknowledge us. My dear people, we are already the children of God, but what we are to be in the future has not yet been revealed; all we know is that when it is revealed we shall be like him because we shall see him as he really is" (1 Jn. 3:1-2).

These and many similar texts formulate the core of the Gospel under its various aspects. (See also, e.g., Jn. 1:1-18; 3:14-17; Acts 2:14-39; Rom. 16:25-27; 1 Cor. 15:1-2; Eph. 1:3-11; 2:1-11; Col. 1:25—2:3; 1 Tim. 1:15-17; 2 Tim. 2:8-13; Tit. 3:3-8).

It is certainly of great value to become aware of these, the main elements that make up the central message of the Gospel. The whole is presented clearly as the outcome of the loving plan of God the Father; it turns finally to his glory (see, e.g., Rom. 16:27; 1 Cor. 15:28; Phil. 2:11; 1 Tim. 1:15-17; Rev. 19:6-8) and our perfect union with him. This plan of the Father's love only becomes known to us by means of the event of our salvation through Christ. The Father sends us his Son; he sends him despite man's continuous rebellion against him when man has made himself utterly unworthy of such a stupendous love.

The great mystery is Christ himself—he the Son and gift of the Father and, at the same time, our brother and Savior. Christ holds this central place precisely because he is "the Christ," sent to us from the Father in a most special way (see, e.g., Jn. 6:68; 16:28; Mt. 16:16; 22:33-44). He alone brings us salvation. "Salvation is to be found through him alone; for there is no one else in the world, whose name God has given to men, by whom we can be saved" (Acts 4:12; see also Jn. 11:51f; Acts 15:11; 1 Tim. 2:5).

Christ achieved his work of salvation mainly by his death and resurrection. In all four Gospels the emphasis clearly rests in the narrative of his passion and resurrection. And from the beginning of the apostolic preaching, we find at its very center the enthusiastic proclamation of the paschal mystery (see, e.g., Acts 2:22-36; 3:13-16; 4:8-12; 5:29-32; 10:39-43; 13:28-31; 17:31; 26:22-23) with its emphasis on the resurrection.

To give testimony as witnesses of the resurrection was considered to be the characteristic task of the apostles. After the apostasy of Judas, they received Matthias into the college of the twelve in order that he might act with them "as witnesses to his (Christ's) resurrection" (Acts 1:22).

The paschal mystery was proclaimed by the apostles not just as a sensational event, but as an event of the greatest possible importance for the life of all men—as a challenge to a new way of life. Through the death and resurrection of his Son, God claims our love and calls us to profound change in our lives.

This interpretation of the Christ event already stands out in the first proclamation of the resurrection. After St. Peter's speech at Pentecost which laid such stress on the resurrection, his listeners were "cut to the heart and said to Peter and the apostles: 'What must we do, brothers?' 'You must repent,' Peter answered, 'and every one of you must be baptized in the name of Jesus Christ for the forgiveness of your sins, and you will receive the Holy Spirit' " (Acts 2:37f; see also 3:19; 5:31; 9:6; 11:19; 26:19f).

In Peter's fundamental statement at Pentecost, we already encounter the threefold unity which is so characteristic of the apostolic preaching: faith in Jesus Christ which includes conversion, baptism, and the Holy Spirit. In baptism God gives us his Spirit which makes us one with Christ and lets us share his life. As one with Christ in the Holy Spirit, we are his community—the Church.

The Church as the work of the Holy Spirit has a very prominent place in the apostolic preaching and even more so in the religious experience of the early Christians. On the one hand, we find great stress upon the social dimensions of salvation; on the other, we encounter a "Pentecostal" experience of the Church as a "confraternity" of love and of prayer. The first Christians were deeply aware of their new type of prayer, so characterized by its dynamism. The Holy Spirit let them join in prayer with Christ, and in union with Christ the prayer expressed especially their filial attitude toward God (see, e.g., Gal. 4:4-6; Rom. 8:15).

The way the Church is presented in the New Testament surely does not allow us to think of it as an amorphic mob of enthusiasts. The doctrinal and pastoral leadership of the apostles is stressed unmistakably. The Christians considered themselves to be the community of the risen Lord. They were, above all, a community of faith. They knew themselves to be one by their faith in the same God and Father in heaven, in the same Lord and Savior Jesus Christ and in the same baptism and Holy Spirit (see Eph. 4:3-4) to whom they owed both their unity as a single body and their incomparable religious vigor.

Here on earth this community of the risen Lord already saw itself as the people of the new covenant, "a chosen race, a royal priesthood, a consecrated nation, a people set apart to sing the praises of God" (1 Pet. 2:9). The early Christians were well aware that their call demanded from them a new kind of life, very different from the life they had lived before their conversion (see, e.g., Eph. 2:1-10; 4:1-3; 5:1-2; Col. 3:12-17; Rom. 6:4).

But this new life here on earth was only the beginning of a life that would be consummated in glory. With unwavering hope and burning desire, the early Christians expected the second coming of the Lord. "For us our homeland is heaven, and from heaven comes the Savior we are waiting for, the Lord Jesus Christ, and he will transfigure these wretched bodies of ours into copies of his glorious body. He will do that by the same power with which he can subdue the whole universe" (Phil. 3:20f; see also Acts 3:20f; Rom. 8:23; 1 Cor. 15:23-28; Col. 3:1-4; 2 Tim. 4:8; Tit. 2:13; Heb. 11:13). The New Testament, which echoes the preaching of the apostles in a unique way, closes significantly with this expression of the hope of the early Church: "The one who guarantees these revelations repeats his promise: I shall indeed be with you soon. Amen! Come, Lord Jesus" (Rev. 22:20).

Characteristic Aspects of the Gospel Message

In the first section of this chapter we have seen that it is not enough to present the doctrines of the Gospel without theological error; it is at least equally important that this presentation show lucidly the main idea of the whole Gospel and the special character of Christian revelation. Any catechesis that does not fulfill this basic demand risks the danger of disfiguring the Christian message. What, then, are some of the most outstanding themes of the Gospel message which help us in particular to understand its meaning and special character?

The Gospel is, above all, a *message of love* which demands a response of love from us. Only by a life of love can we satisfy the loving invitation of God. His plan of salvation materializes, in fact, as a great drama of love in which God and men are the chief actors. God planned and started it, and, in spite of the failures of men, it will lead to the final triumph of his overwhelming love. In order to depict this triumph in all its greatness, we must also depict graphically the unworthiness, weakness and resistance of man together with the reality and malice of sin.

God challenges man by his invitation. The Christian message is by its nature at once both joyful tidings—a real "Gospel"—and a *challenge* which demands a radical decision by man. Man has no other alternative than a grateful acceptance of this friendship offered to him. To refuse would mean the final loss of everything that matters in his human existence. The Gospel must be accepted wholeheartedly; it demands a basic conversion ultimately consisting in liberation from selfish concern for oneself. The entire Gospel can be summed up in the words of our Lord: "The time has come and the Kingdom of God is near. Turn away from your sins and believe the Good News" (Mk. 1:15).

In the Gospel message, we must distinguish clearly, so to speak, three dimensions. The totality of the Gospel is the loving design of *God* which has *Christ* as its very center and is intended for the good of *man*, its recipient.

Viewing the beginning and the end, the divine design is clearly *Father-centered* (God-centered.) It comes from the very depths of the Father's love. He achieves his plan of salvation by sending us his Son. The Son acts in the name of the Father. At the end of his work of redemption the Son "will hand over the kingdom to God the Father . . . so that God may be all in all" (1 Cor. 15:24-28).

Viewing the primary means by which God had revealed his love to us and made it a reality in our midst, the Christian message is *Christ-centered*. Christ is the most perfect expression and the most convincing proof of the Father's love (see, e.g., Jn. 3:16f; Rom. 8:32; 1 Jn. 4:8-11). Since Christ has manifested himself as the outstanding envoy, the anointed one of the Father, as the way to the Father (Jn. 14:6) and the unique mediator between God and man (1 Tim. 2:5; see also Jn. 3:17; 4:42; 11:52), any type of catechesis or worship that stops with Christ and does not ascend with him to the Father contradicts the Gospel.

Viewing the beneficiary of the Christian message, the Gospel can rightly be called *man-centered*. All of God's revelation and the whole work of salvation are meant for man. Vatican II has, in a special way, stressed this human dimension of divine revelation and salvation. Because of its great importance for evangelization, we shall treat this dimension in more detail in a later chapter.

The Rest of the Christian Message

In the evangelization of the early Church we find an exemplary emphasis on the core of the Christian message, but we do not find there any indication that the rest does not count or may be disregarded. On the contrary, we meet with a strong reaction from the apostles against people who questioned truths of the apostolic preaching, even though these truths did not belong to the center of the Christian religion. This can be seen in 1 John 4:2f.

Under the influence of a faulty gnosis, a movement of spiritual enlightenment, some Christians thought that Christ did not really become man but appeared among us with a seeming body. These Christians did not deny our salvation through Christ or his transcendent dignity. Nevertheless, the condemnation of their error is definitive—they lack the Spirit of God.

We find the same condemnation in St. Paul. Significant examples are his rejection of a faulty asceticism (Col. 2:16-23) and especially his vehement condemnation of those who after the clear decision of the apostles still insisted upon the necessity of circumcision (see, e.g., Gal. 5:7-12). In these cases there was no denial of the center of the Christian message, but the apostles were aware of how these errors endangered the center of the Christian faith. They rightly saw in these errors a falsification of God's plan of salvation.

From the New Testament, that normative model of genuine evangelization, we also learn the basic principles for properly integrating the less central doctrines into the proclamation of God's Word:

1. The less central doctrines have a function of service to the more central ones; they help us to understand better and more fully God's plan of salvation.

2. They must be presented with the correct emphasis due their position in the context of the whole Christian message. Any overemphasis necessarily diverts attention from the center to the periphery. To speak more of guardian angels than of divine providence, more of the souls in purgatory than of repentance, more of the Blessed Mother than of the Holy Spirit, disfigures the Christian message.

3. These doctrines must never be denied. But in an initial evangelization, it may be better to omit them than to risk not implanting with sufficient force the central truths. Here many modern "evangelists" still have a great deal to learn from the apostolic preaching. In catechesis we often bring "too much too early."

4. The relationship of these doctrines to the center of Christian revelation must be clearly shown. If in a particular case the connection cannot be made clear, since it surpasses the capacity of those being evangelized, it is better to delay teaching of the doctrine until presentation can result in clear understanding. For example, to present children of seven years with an explicit teaching on original sin or on the immaculate conception will serve more to confuse than to help them.

Chapter Six
Evangelization
and Sacramental Life

The core of the Christian message is the saving love of God revealed and given to us through Jesus Christ. More than anything else, God wishes to establish a union of life and love with man, that is, with each individual man and with the human community. This plan of God can be implemented only through a community that worships God in spirit and in truth (cf. Jn. 4:23f). The deep commitment of faith by which this community of followers of Jesus must be distinguished necessarily leads to adoration in the Spirit.

Yet what do we find in the Church today but an ever increasing number of people who have been baptized but who are not at all committed to a Christian life? Who can deny that such an alarming situation contradicts the saving plan of God? We all know that the primitive Church and after it the ancient Church of the martyrs was a deeply committed community. How then did it arrive at today's scandalous situation?

One of the main reasons, as it is commonly admitted, is the defective administration of the sacraments. In the lapse of centuries, the sacraments increasingly were administered without a companion emphasis on evangelization. The emphasis once placed upon evangelization was shifted to the sacramental ministry alone. The present situation, however, cannot be remedied without a careful rethinking of the interrelation between evangelization and the sacraments.

*The Place of Evangelization and Sacraments
in the Christian Life*

The New Testament witnesses convincingly to the close connection between the primitive apostolic preaching and the Church's sacramental life from the very beginning. Matthew's account of how Christ sent out the apostles tells us clearly what the apostolic Church understood as its main task: "Go, therefore, make disciples of all the nations; baptize them . . . and teach them to observe all the commands I gave you" (Mt. 28:19f). The first evangelization leads to sacramental life, and after the reception of the first sacrament, Christian formation has to be continued by further preaching of the Gospel.

We find the same emphasis in the Acts of the Apostles on the original practice of the Church. The first pastoral directive of Peter at Pentecost leaves no doubt about this. After his talk, a model of eloquent evangelization, his listeners ask Peter what they must do to be saved. His answer is terse: "You must repent, and every one of you must be baptized in the name of Jesus Christ for the forgiveness of your sins, and you will receive the gift of the Holy Spirit" (Acts 2:41).

Luke does not forget to mention that after their baptism the new Christians "spent their time in learning from the apostles, taking part in the fellowship, and sharing in the fellowship meals and in the prayers" (Acts 2:42). When Luke mentions the fellowship meals, we may with good reason think of a eucharistic celebration in the setting of an ordinary meal.

In any case, the first evangelization leads to Christian initiation by the sacrament and the neophytes then mature in their Christian life through the guidance and instruction they receive from the apostles. This close connection of evangelization with baptism, the basic sacrament, is manifested in many texts of the Acts of the Apostles and the Epistles (see, e.g., Acts 8:12; 8:26-38; 9:17-19; 10:34-48; 16:32f; 19:1-7; 1 Cor. 1:14-17).

A short time later when the eucharistic celebration had received its commonly accepted form, the liturgy of the word prepared for the liturgy of the Eucharist. The first evangelization and the catechesis that followed led to a new life that started with the sacraments of initiation and later on was increasingly deepened by the sacraments, especially by the regular celebration of the Eucharist.

In this way evangelization and the sacraments have, according to the plan of God, an important and irreplaceable role in the work of salvation. They require and complement one another. The first evangelization leads to the first commitment of faith, the catechesis that follows deepens the commitment more and more, and the committed faith is the indispensable condition for receiving the sacraments fruitfully.

The sacraments, for their part, express and complete the commitment of faith; they signify and at the same time confer divine life, God's personal communication to man. Since preconciliar theology and catechesis did not sufficiently stress this relationship, the Council emphasized it with this important statement: "The sacraments not only presuppose faith, but by means of words and objects they also nourish, strengthen and express it; that is why they are called 'sacraments of faith' " (*Constitution on the Sacred Liturgy*, no. 59).

By these words the Council intended to correct the error that the sacraments to a certain extent, at least in some difficult situations, could replace the commitment of faith. In order to interpret the Council's words correctly, we must keep in mind that "faith" is to be understood in the same way that Vatican II described it in the *Constitution on Divine Revelation* (no. 5)— as not only the full submission of the intellect but also man's free giving "of his whole self to God" (see also the General Catechetical Directory, no. 56).

In the normal case, committed faith must be actualized through the reception of the sacraments. We have already seen how Peter insisted from the beginning of Christian evangelization upon baptism as the necessary condition for salvation (cf. Acts 2:38; see also Mt. 28:19; Mk. 16:16; Jn. 3:5).

Why does God's plan of salvation require the reception of the sacraments? The reason is obvious. Salvation must be received and experienced as the undeserved gift of God. Faith, too, is of course the gift of God. Nevertheless, since faith is our personal free decision, we experience it more as our own contribution in the work of redemption. It is indeed our response, although under the influence of God's grace, to his loving invitation.

However, when we receive the sacrament, we are totally aware of ourselves as the undeserving recipients of God's life. The Divine Lover, like anyone who loves, wants us to experience the gift of his love. By means of the sacramental sign, man can perceive and experience in his own way the invisible gift of salvation that he receives in the sacrament. This results from his personal encounter with Christ the Savior.

The sacraments are our saving encounters with Christ. He himself acts in the administration and reception of each sacrament. Provided that the sacraments are duly explained, administered and received, they lead to a profound experience of our union with Christ. They have been instituted with the intention of letting us experience salvation as the great gift that results from our personal encounter with Christ.

All these reasons help us to understand why God insists that the commitment of faith be actualized through the reception of the sacraments. At the same time, however, they show clearly that the sacraments cannot be considered an alternative to faith but only as its actualization and completion. Their task is to convey to us the experience of salvation and of our saving union with God that comes from faith.

What counts most in the salvation of adults is always faith and not the reception of the sacrament. Faith is the element that is totally indispensable. Whenever the reception of the sacrament is impossible, the commitment of faith can always replace the life-giving function of the sacrament, although not its juridical effects.

Conversely, in the salvation of adults, the reception of the sacrament can never replace the necessity of faith. "It is impossible to please God without faith, since anyone who comes to him must believe that he exists and rewards those who try to find him" (Heb. 11:6). That faith in cases of necessity can substitute for the actual reception of the sacrament we have in fact always admitted, at least implicitly, with the saving power we ascribed to baptism of desire.

Whoever sincerely places the preeminence of faith in the

work of salvation over the reception of the sacraments must, to be consistent, place the preeminence of evangelization over the administration of the sacraments. The commitment of faith presupposes evangelization just as the reception of the sacraments requires their administration: "Everyone who calls on the name of the Lord will be saved. But they will not ask his help unless they believe in him, and they will not believe in him unless they have heard of him, and will not hear of him unless they get a preacher, and they will never get a preacher unless one is sent. But as Scripture says, 'The footsteps of those who bring good news are a welcome sound' " (Rom. 10:13ff).

When we speak of the preeminence of faith, we do not wish to state a preeminence of faith according to its interior value. Under that aspect we can with good reasons speak of a preeminence of the sacramental act. In a sacrament, even more than in an act of faith, we receive a personal communication of God's life-giving love. If the act of faith is already God's gift and work within us, a sacrament is even more so, provided, of course, that we take into consideration not only the exterior rite but also the interior saving effects of the sacraments.

The act of faith is, above all, an act of man, although done under the influence of God's saving power; in itself, it is a human and not a divine act. Each sacrament, on the contrary, signifies God's saving act which is actualized through this sign. When a sacrament is received with the commitment of faith, God himself works for the salvation of the faithful recipient and communicates with him in the most intimate manner.

The preeminence of faith, therefore, means only a preeminence in the practical order; it means that actual faith is more important than actual reception of the sacraments. This has always been admitted, at least in theory, in Catholic theology.

It is also all that is needed in order to establish the pastoral preeminence of evangelization over the administration of the sacraments. Correct and intensive evangelization can by itself lead to fervent reception of the sacraments, but correct and intensive administration of the sacraments does not by itself lead to a commitment of faith which in the Christian life of adults is even more necessary for salvation.

In the light of these principles, which found clear expression in the doctrine and practice of the early Church, a question is obviously arising: How then was it possible that over the course of Christian history, a gradual shift of emphasis from evangelization to administration of the sacraments took place? In order to understand this shift, we must become aware of the tendency to ritualism which is a common phenomenon of human religious behavior.

The Trend to Ritualism

In the religious behavior of man, we almost always find two constituent elements—one, the interior commitment to God, and the other, the expression of this commitment by exterior signs such as words, gestures and actions. Common religious experience tells us that an appropriate exterior rite can contribute much in facilitating and deepening interior commitment. It is obvious that the interior element is the decisive one which in the end determines the religious value, but the exterior element is also important.

In most cases the exterior element is necessary because of the nature of man as a body-person and as a social being. As a body-person, man needs the "incarnation" of his religion for himself, and as a social being he needs the exterior expression for his corporate worship and for communication of his religion to others.

In the Christian religion we understand the interior element to be our faithful and loving commitment to God. By this we respond to God who through his Son has invited us to a union of life and love. Our commitment of faith and love demands from us a profound change in our life (as explained in Chapters Two and Three in this book). The more an act of religion actualizes our commitment of faith and our willingness to change our life, the greater is its religious value.

That such a commitment is not easy for fallen man is obvious to everyone who tries to live it. It takes more than just occasional religious sentiments; it calls for a total surrender to God in the midst of all the distractions and temptations of this world. Christ spoke out clearly and unmistakably about the hard road that his disciples would have to travel and of the narrow gate that his followers would have to enter (cf. Mt. 7:13f). There can be no doubt that in a truly Christian life, the interior element of generous and unconditional commitment is more difficult than the exterior expression of religion.

In all our human activity, we have a natural tendency to avoid the difficult and to replace it, if possible, with something easier. Because of this, man has a propensity for replacing the difficult element of total commitment and conversion with other, easier elements such as sentiments, gestures and various exterior rites. Such an inclination is entirely natural and human; we should not be at all surprised at such an obvious propensity.

Nevertheless, religious educators, leaders and pastors must be aware of this innate inclination of man. Precisely because of this inclination, true religious education must continuously insist upon the preeminence of the interior element. Christ proclaimed the primacy of the interior element in religion as a criterion of true messianic piety: "In your prayer do not rattle on like the pagans. They think they will win a hearing by the sheer multiplication of words" (Mt. 6:7).

In the ancient Church we can easily find a correct balance between evangelization and sacramental life. But in the Middle Ages when entire tribes together accepted Christianity, the initial evangelization became rather superficial. Thousands received baptism because their leader, the duke or chieftain did so, without sufficiently understanding its meaning and, therefore, without any real change in their lives. Even after receiving baptism, they were given little instruction.

Furthermore, the eucharistic celebrations of the Middle Ages were no longer distinguished by their great evangelizing power as those of the ancient Church had been. The liturgy was no longer celebrated in the language of the congregation. The religious instruction given inside and outside of the liturgy left much to be desired with regard to quantity and even more with regard to evangelizing quality. In such an unfavorable environment, a ritualism spread which increasingly affected the sacramental life and the piety of Christians. Eventually, this undeniable ritualism provoked the radical and exaggerated reaction of the Protestant reformers.

Within the Catholic Church, the Council of Trent vigorously eliminated the more shocking forms of medieval ritualism and at the same time insisted on a solid, fundamental catechesis. But in spite of its great merits, the Tridentine reform was unable to restore the ancient balance between evangelization and sacramental life.

Because of its defensive attitude toward the Protestant reformers, the Council overemphasized the sacramental aspect in the work of redemption and did not adequately stress the fundamental importance of the commitment of faith in the whole process of salvation. The sacraments were no longer seen as organically connected with the life of faith. Post-Tridentine theology and catechesis were concerned before all else with the juridical requirements of the sacramental sign and its causal connection with the sacramental effect, and not, at least primarily, with the saving function of the sacraments and its indispensable connection to the commitment and life of faith.

Because of this basic attitude, post-Tridentine catechesis was more interested in the dogmatic, ritual and juridical details of the particular sacraments than in the life of faith as the foundation of all the sacraments of life. And when faith was considered, the great stress was placed on the "true" faith in the meaning of doctrinal orthodoxy and not so much on the total commitment of oneself, which in the final analysis gives to faith its religious value. All of this emphasis contributed to an unbalanced form of sacramentalism which did not do justice to the fundamental role of evangelization.

Because of its sacramental attitude in the sense we ascribe to it, the post-Tridentine Church failed to solve the urgent problem of a more appropriate administration of the sacraments of initiation, that is, baptism, confirmation and the Eucharist.

The Problem of the Sacraments of Initiation

One of the main historical reasons why the Church gradually came to adopt an unfavorable sacramentalism seems to have been a defective administration of the sacraments of initiation which developed over the course of time.

If we understand the Church of the apostles and early Christians to be the "ecclesia," that is, the community of those who have been called, then the Church by its very nature is a community of committed people. It is not the call itself that makes people members of this community but the response to this call, the commitment of faith which finds its solemn expression in the sacraments of initiation.

These sacraments form a close unit and constitute the solemn rite of Christian initiation. In the ancient Church they were received on one and the same night, usually the night before Easter or Pentecost, and after a long and intensive preparation. The Christians saw in them the definitive expression of their faith and, at the same time, the visible acceptance of their faith by God and its consecration in the mysteries of initiation. In that way they experienced from the beginning of their Christian lives the close connection between their commitment of faith and the sacraments.

Almost certainly, from the time of the apostles, Christian parents brought their children to be baptized. The baptism of these children was appreciated as a special privilege for the parents who, of course, committed themselves to providing Christian instruction for their children and thus leading them gradually to make their own commitment of faith. Provided that such baptism is clearly understood as a privilege of truly committed Christian parents or other responsible Christian educators and is limited to such cases, there is no pastoral difficulty in this "apostolic" custom, especially if steps are later taken to help parents meet this obligation.

However, serious problems arise if children of uncommitted parents share the same privilege and even more so if the other sacraments of initiation are received without any personal commitment of faith. That means, in effect, that we accept the Christian religion primarily as a matter of ritual.

And today, in actual fact, countless infants are baptized without any true commitment on the part of their parents to provide them with a solid Christian education. In many cases the parents are simply incapable of providing such education. If they do make such a promise, it is merely a formality. Even where the children are later sent to a Catholic school or take part in a parish religion program, more often than not they fail to achieve a genuine Christian commitment because of the irreligious atmosphere of the home and the rather limited evangelizing power of our current religious education programs.

First Communion and the eucharistic celebrations that are held in the setting of a school activity do little to change the situation. At the age of First Communion, children are not yet capable of making a mature commitment. During their participation in a parish or school religion program, they may have learned much about religion, but they have never been evangelized.

Confirmation simply adds to the damage, since this third sacrament of initiation is also received before children are sufficiently mature to make an authentic personal commitment. Thus we have the alarming situation where the end of religious instruction invariably brings the end of their participation in the life of the Church and of their own prayer life as well. They are surely not committed Christians, and without further evangelization they never will be.

This is the way that the vast majority of Christians are brought into the Christian community. They make no true commitment of their own. They have never decided to be or to become Christians. In the ages of a monolithic Christian culture and society with strong Christian convictions on the part of the group as a whole, such an initiation may have been sufficient and usually resulted in no disastrous consequences. In our age of religious indifference, pluralism and subjectivism, it certainly will not work any longer. However, we should waste no time in criticism of past ages; rather, we must find workable solutions to the problems of today.

Before Vatican II many people viewed the Church primarily as an institution. We still insist today on her institutional character and her God-willed juridical structure. But in company with the Bible and Vatican II, we now consider her primarily as a communion of faith, love and life. One timely paragraph in the General Catechetical Directory makes this important statement: "The Church is a communion. She herself acquired a fuller awareness of that truth in the Second Vatican Council" (no. 66).

Whoever sees the Church primarily as a juridical entity will in consequence stress above all the ritual and juridical aspects of initiation and fail to give due emphasis to personal commitment. But whoever considers the Church primarily as the committed assembly of God's children—the community of the "faithful"—will logically demand a solemn expression of personal commitment as a constitutive element of authentic initiation. Without this, the rite is meaningless. You cannot enter a deeply committed community without personal commitment.

For these reasons we insist that at least one sacrament of initiation be conferred at a time when young people have sufficient appreciation of the true meaning and importance of Christian life and are mature enough to commit themselves to live it forever. The obvious choice here is confirmation.

If true commitment is expected, then confirmation could hardly be administered before the end of adolescence. By postponing confirmation to that time we would obtain a badly needed opportunity for real evangelization of these young people. We would also be responding to a well-founded demand from modern youth who wish to make their own choice about Church membership.

The religious program before confirmation would, of course, be focused on the solemn personal decision that would accompany reception of the sacrament. All formation up to this point would, in fact, be part of an ongoing initiation that finally terminates in the sacramental commitment.

The administration of the other sacraments would also, in such a program, need reform. In many places a pre-baptismal catechesis of the parents is now a requirement before their child's ceremony—and this is a minimum which responsible pastors must require. To baptize infants whose parents do not sincerely commit themselves to educate their children in a Christian manner is, in fact, forbidden. How can we speak of a serious commitment by parents who are unwilling to present themselves for minimal instruction about their obligation?

Moreover, we must remember that such pre-baptismal instruction is only a first step in this necessary reform. We must find ways to help parents, the responsible educators, to achieve a truly Christian life. The promises made by parents remain an empty formality if not even one of the parents is living up to his or her Christian commitment.

We can hardly expect children at the time of their First Communion to make a commitment in the strict meaning of the word, since this would be far beyond their capacity. But the preparatory catechesis at this time must be outstanding for its evangelizing quality. Any kind of formalism and ritualism must carefully be avoided, and the children must be led to the initial commitment that can be expected at their age.

Since the child's commitment is still imperfect, his parents, the responsible educators, must commit themselves to continue his Christian education until maturity. Previously before First Communion, we demanded only that children have the necessary understanding of the sacrament. Today, however, First Communion should not be permitted without sufficient guarantee that a normal continuation of eucharistic life will take place thereafter. Obviously, this requires more than occasional mechanical communions after the first one. We were definitely too much concerned in the past with First Communion and not enough with the eucharistic life that should follow.

Answers to Some Difficulties

Some readers may feel that our presentation of the connection between faith and the sacraments hardly does justice to the basic principle of Catholic sacramental theology by which the sacraments produce their saving effect—"ex opere operato"—and not just in virtue of man's own good actions. As is well known, the Council of Trent solemnly defined this key point of Catholic teaching in response to the Protestant reformers who saw in the sacraments only important signs of man's faith. The

Protestants did not deny the usefulness and even the necessity of baptism and the Eucharist, the two "basic sacraments" they retained. However, they considered these sacraments to be simply a very special expression of faith; it is the faith thus expressed which, they believed, makes man accepted by God. The sacraments are appreciated as outstanding manifestations of the faith which Christ himself laid down for his community.

Of course, Catholics also see the sacraments as manifestations of faith, and this aspect was deliberately stressed anew by the Vatican Council. But the Church sees more than mere signs of faith in the sacraments; it sees them primarily as signs of God's saving love by which God, beyond any merits of man, graciously responds to man's faith by accepting him into a union of life and love with himself.

For the Protestant the sacraments are primarily acts of man who believes; for the Catholic they are primarily the saving gift of God which man receives in faith. For the Protestant the sacraments mean man's faithful "yes" to God who saves; for the Catholic they mean, above all, God's coming to man who believes. We are enriched; we "receive" the sacraments. This, of course, calls for a truly human reception that always involves man's own free activity.

By the expression "ex opere operato" the Council of Trent wanted to describe more specifically the way in which the sacraments lead to salvation. The gift of God's life and love that we receive first in baptism and then more intensively in the other sacraments is not given to us as a reward for any merit on our part, something that we could in some way claim as "recompense" promised to us. We receive this as a free and undeserved gift of God's self-communication. This does not in any way mean that faith is not required for the reception of this gift. It is required, however, as a necessary condition and disposition and not as a merit (or meritorious act) which claims its reward.

The case is different when we consider the actualization of our faith by prayer and works of charity. According to numerous texts of the Bible (see, e.g., Mt. 5:11; 16:27; Rom. 2:6; 2 Tim. 4:8; 2 Jn. 8; Rev. 2:23; 14:13; 22:12), works of faith are rewarded by God communicating himself with increasing intensity to the man who acts by faith. In the language of scholastic theology we say that such actualization of our faith produces its saving effect "ex opere operantis," that is, the actualization of faith by its very nature unites the man of faith more intensely with God and lets him share more perfectly in God's own life.

In the fury of religious controversy, the Catholic and Protestant positions have usually been presented in such a manner as to leave no room for a common understanding of the two positions. We failed to examine the different formulations with sufficient care to see that they were two different aspects of God's saving plan which in themselves do not exclude but rather complement one another. The seemingly unbridgeable gulf can be bridged provided that Catholics, in accord with Vatican II, stress that all the sacraments presuppose faith and that Protestants acknowledge in the sacraments the manifestation and experience of God's saving love.

Our insistence upon administering the sacraments only to Christians who have been sufficiently evangelized may give the impression of offending against the acknowledged pastoral principle that the sacraments are for man and not man for the sacraments. No sincere pastor would ever deny this sound principle. It means that the sacraments are not an end in themselves but a God-given means for the salvation of man.

In cases of necessity where we are not certain if someone is capable or disposed to receive a sacrament and there is no way to make sure, we take the risk and administer the sacrament. For example, in case of a sudden accident where we find a Catholic unconscious, we presume the necessary disposition for repentance and give him the sacrament of the sick.

However, in cases where it is possible to ascertain the necessary disposition, we are obviously obliged to do so. Omitting it would be to risk harmful ritualism. Medicines, we all agree, are for man and not man for medicines, but that does not mean we are allowed to neglect the necessary conditions for obtaining their desired effect. Some drugs are meant to be taken in the morning before breakfast; you cannot say, "Medicines are for man and not man for medicines," and take them after dinner.

The Evangelizing Power of the Sacraments

The sacraments "presuppose faith" (*Constitution on the Sacred Liturgy*, no. 59) and faith supposes evangelization. Evangelization, therefore, has to precede and prepare for the sacraments. Yet, at the same time, the sacraments, if celebrated properly, have great evangelizing power. Existential experience of God and further deepening of faith is to be intended in the administration and reception of the sacraments.

Post-Tridentine sacramental theology usually considered the sacraments almost exclusively under the ritual aspect of valid and licit administration or the theological aspect of the effect produced in virtue of the sacramental power ("ex opere operato") in the recipient. It badly neglected the educational aspects of the sacraments, which had been stressed, again almost exclusively, by the Protestants.

Vatican II made a great contribution by its emphasis on the educational contribution of the sacraments to existentially express and to deepen faith. The statement of the *Constitution on the Sacred Liturgy* is very clear and precise: "Because they are signs the sacraments also instruct. They not only presuppose faith, but by words and signs they also nourish, strengthen and express it; that is why they are called 'sacraments of faith.' They do indeed impart grace, but in addition the very act of celebrating them disposes the faithful most effectively to receive this grace in a fruitful manner, to worship God reverently and to practice charity. It is therefore of capital importance that the faithful easily understand the sacramental signs, and with great eagerness have frequent recourse to those sacraments which were instituted to nourish the Christian life" (no. 59).

In order to restore to the sacraments and to the whole liturgy the due educational function and power, the Council laid down "norms based upon the educational and pastoral nature of the liturgy" (*Constitution on the Sacred Liturgy*, nos. 33-44). In the new regulations issued since the Council, the liturgy of the sacraments has been inspired throughout by this desire to actualize as fully as possible the evangelizing potential in the celebration of each sacrament.

There are two basic differences between the sacramental effect which a sacrament produces in a properly disposed recipient, and the educational effect produced through proper celebration of a sacrament. The sacramental effect is conferred only on the person who receives the sacrament; the educational effect, however, may be perceived by all who participate faithfully in the celebration of the sacrament. Indeed, the effect may sometimes be much deeper for those Christians assisting at a celebration than for the recipient himself. The most extreme example of this would occur in the baptism of infants. The child himself is still incapable of expressing faith and of growing in it. But a properly celebrated baptismal rite is supposed to be a deep experience of faith for all who assist at it.

The sacramental effect is produced in virtue of the sacrament which someone received with the necessary disposition of faith. It does not depend on the manner of celebration as such. The educational effect, on the other hand, depends completely on the manner of celebration.

What we mean by the evangelizing power of the sacraments and how it can be actualized will be explained more fully in the next chapter with the example of the most sublime and central sacrament, the Eucharist. Not only in the Eucharist but in each sacrament, the evangelizing effect of the particular celebration depends essentially upon the faith-experience of Christ's saving presence and action and in the ever deeper commitment to Christ in our whole life that results from it.

Chapter Seven
Evangelizing Power
of the Eucharist

According to the preparatory text of the last Synod of Bishops, it is by means of evangelization that the Church makes Christ present to men today and challenges them to accept him as "the foundation of man's entire hope" (*The Evangelization of the Modern World*, Washington 1973, p. 1).

If we take evangelization in this broader sense and not simply as the proclamation of the Gospel to persons who have never made a true commitment of faith, then certainly the celebration of the Eucharist has a valuable contribution to make. For those already baptized and initiated into the life of faith, it is, of course, the ordinary and most important means of an ongoing and ever more thorough evangelization.

However, we must stress from the very beginning that this evangelizing power is not something that works "ex opere operato" as an inevitable effect of valid consecration; rather, it depends entirely on the way the Eucharist is celebrated and whether the participants make use of the excellent opportunities offered for authentic evangelization.

Evangelizing Task of the Eucharist

The Eucharist is aimed at evangelization. By insisting that its evangelizing power does not result automatically from the "valid" use of the power of consecration, we do not in any way intend to deny that Christ in fact instituted the Eucharist to evangelize his community. Rather, we want to stress that any eucharistic celebration that does not evangelize is plainly deficient since it does not fulfill the intention of Christ in instituting the Eucharist.

This will become obvious if we consider the basic elements of the sacrament. Christ instituted the Eucharist at his farewell supper with the apostles, the inner circle of his community. He wanted to provide more comfort for them during the time they would be deprived of his presence until he would come again (cf. 1 Cor. 11:26), so he bestowed the great privilege of an invisible yet real and saving encounter with him.

The Lord indeed remains always with his Church (cf. Mt. 28:20; Jn. 15:1-5), but his presence, though real and veiled in mystery, must be continually remembered, reaffirmed and celebrated by his community, so that it becomes a saving reality within the Church. This is the very aim of the Eucharist: it must be celebrated as *an encounter of Christ with his community.* Here he reminds them of their Christian vocation and commitment, consoles them amid the trials of their journey, strengthens them in their fight against the powers of evil, encourages them to live according to his Gospel and awakens in them a deep longing for his coming in glory.

In each eucharistic celebration that really meets the expectations of the Lord, the faithful for their part reassert his saving presence and, like the apostles after his resurrection, gather around him. His presence leads them to a new and deeper awareness of their Christian vocation and their saving mission in the world of today.

In this joyful encounter they once again acknowledge the glorious Christ as Lord of their own lives and of the whole world. From Christ himself they again accept the good news of salvation and know themselves to be personally sent by Christ to bring to the whole world Christ's peace—in a word, his Gospel.

We cannot say, of course, that since the liturgical renewal we always experience such an intensive encounter with Christ in each eucharistic celebration. But no one can deny these three points—that the Eucharist is aimed at this according to the Lord's intention, that priests have a serious obligation to strive for this encounter between Christ and his community in the eucharistic celebration, and that the Eucharist will be an evangelizing force in the measure that its celebration provides an encounter with Christ.

We should justly feel ashamed that for so long a time we indulged in a kind of rubricism, more concerned with ceremonies than with giving to the whole celebration its full expression of Christ's encounter with his pilgrim community. True, we encounter Christ in all the sacraments and not only in the Eucharist, but the special element of our encounter with him here is precisely "Eucharist," that is, our thanksgiving in union with him.

In the first part of the Mass we proclaim "the marvels of God" (Acts 2:11) which have their center in the saving love of God as revealed in Jesus Christ. To these marvels, we respond in the second part of the Mass with the liturgy of the Eucharist. Thus, each eucharistic liturgy, if celebrated authentically, makes us aware of the very center of our religion. In each celebration, the main theme is invariably the saving love of God which Christ has conveyed to us.

In each eucharistic celebration we also commit ourselves solemnly to a life according to the Gospel, which is our only appropriate response to God's overwhelming love. Provided we take the celebration seriously, we cannot celebrate the Eucharist without accepting again and more intensely the Gospel of God's love and then going on to echo it in our lives.

The eucharistic celebration will be further deepened by seeing and celebrating it in the light of the *paschal mystery*. Christ here meets his community for the purpose of drawing it into the mystery of his passion, death and resurrection. Not only do we share abundantly in the fruits of Christ's redeeming work; he also summons us to share actively in the total surrender of love to his heavenly Father which characterized his whole life and was consummated by his passion and death.

The more we share, through our personal commitment, in the self-surrender of love that constitutes his redeeming sacrifice on the cross and makes it so meritorious, the more we share in the reward by which the heavenly Father acknowledged Christ's

filial obedience on the cross. In this way we proclaim and celebrate in each Eucharist the death and resurrection of our Lord.

Not only that, but we can personally and spiritually reac-
tualize the mystery in ourselves! Anyone who truly participates
in the eucharistic celebration cannot help but be aware of the
nucleus of the Gospel, and any authentic eucharistic celebration
requires that the community proclaim again the saving love of
God, accept that love and with his help actualize it in their lives.
Is this not the precise aim of evangelization?

The same idea can be presented in a different way. After
the continuous rebellious "no" of Adam's lineage, the second
Adam, Christ, by his obedience and loving "yes" on the cross,
established the new covenant of friendship between God and
man. As a covenant of friendship, it requires by its very nature
that all who belong to it must ratify it by a personal commitment of lasting loyalty and the love of friendship.

Even Christ our Savior cannot make us friends of God
unless we personally ratify the pact of friendship that he established on the cross. It is precisely in the Eucharist that Christians ratify the covenant which Christ there established and
which the Father accepted and ratified in the resurrection and
exaltation of his Son. The covenant established by Christ in our
name becomes truly and fully our own through the Eucharist.

In this connection two points deserve special attention.
First, in the Eucharist, the community of Christ not only
commits itself to proclaim the saving plan of God; it also
commits itself to make this loving plan a reality in the world of
today.

Second, the plan of God aims at a total salvation of the
whole man and not just a "spiritual" salvation which would
shamefully disregard man's liberation and development of the
temporal level (see Chapter Eight). Without the temporal commitment of the Christian community, its Gospel of salvation
lacks credibility. As we have said, the evangelizing effect of the
Eucharist does not come from the sacramental value of the
celebration as such, nor from its faultless rubrical performance,
but from the depth and sincerity of the Christian community's
commitment, convincingly expressed in the celebration and vig-

orously carried out in the life of the community.

We cannot deny that in the past, because of deficient formation and celebration, many Christians of good will were more concerned, for example, with the liberation of souls from purgatory than with the total salvation of their neighbors. They were not sufficiently aware that every eucharistic celebration helps the souls in purgatory apart from any specific intention in this regard, but the total salvation of our neighbor will not be achieved without a particular and sincere commitment on our part. Hence, Christ expects us to dedicate ourselves unselfishly to the well-being of those around us and not concentrate primarily on the souls of the departed.

To enable us to do this, Christ communicates his Spirit to us in each Eucharist. We do not yet sufficiently understand and celebrate the Eucharist as an actualization of Pentecost. As in the first Pentecost, Christ in each Eucharist fills his community with the Spirit and sends its members forth to proclaim the message of salvation and to embody it in the world of today. The life of the first Christians, as St. Luke describes it in Acts 2:42-47, gives us the model of authentic and powerful evangelization.

The Eucharist of the primitive Church distinguished itself by correct balance between the *temporal and eschatological dimensions.* How deeply were these early Christians longing for the second coming of their Lord in glory. But at the same time they were fully aware that through their life according to the Gospel, they had to prepare the world for that final coming of Christ. If, in some cases, Christians disregarded their temporal commitment, St. Paul reminded them of it quite drastically (cf. 2 Thes. 3:6-11).

The more we reflect upon the evangelizing power of the Eucharist, the more another question arises: How is it possible that so many Eucharists are being celebrated each day without any remarkable evangelizing result? The only satisfactory answer is that actual evangelization does not result from the nature of the Eucharist as such, but from the appropriate celebration of the Eucharist according to its nature.

How To Make the Eucharistic Celebration
a True Evangelization

The recent liturgical renewal is an enormous aid in restoring to the Eucharist its evangelizing power. The new liturgical legislation emphasizes the true meaning and pastoral aim of each liturgical action. Usually it gives us great freedom and offers valuable suggestions for the necessary adaptation to particular situations. The new rubrics have little in common with the old; they are directives rather than fixed rules that exclude meaningful exceptions.

Yet even the best regulations cannot by themselves produce a new spirit. Unfortunately, many liturgical celebrations which exteriorly follow the new regulations lack the new spirit. The effect is a celebration which is not much better than the old. "What gives life is the spirit; the flesh is of no use at all" (Jn. 6:63) is the basic principle stressed by Christ in his first eucharistic catechesis.

What counts most in any liturgical action is that everything —words and actions alike—be really "celebrated." Nothing should be merely recited or performed. Whatever the celebrant or the community says or does must be truly said and done in the spirit of the particular rite. Everything is to be done with an obvious although unobtrusive expression of faith and, thus, of personal involvement, conviction and commitment.

Each word and each action should express a vibration of spirit that animates the whole and creates an atmosphere of deep religious feeling. An authentic celebration avoids, on the one hand, lack of inspiration and, on the other, any theatrical attitude or posture.

Such a celebration makes us deeply aware of Christ's presence during the whole celebration; it disposes us for the renewal of our Christian commitment. In an authentic celebration of the Eucharist, we "experience" ourselves—it is an awareness of faith—united with Christ, consoled, challenged and helped by him.

The behavior of the priestly celebrant is obviously of decisive importance. He has the special privilege and task to present in a visible way the invisible High Priest. Under the influence of the liturgical renewal, many priests today, with genuine religious tact and skill, really help the faithful to experience Christ's presence during the entire celebration. Yet there are other priests who—often without being aware of it themselves— still hinder more than they help.

Here, basically, it is a matter of deep faith by which a priest is able in all sincerity to forget himself and identify with Christ whom he represents. Joyfully he tries to say and do everything in such a manner that Christ can acknowledge this as his own celebration. This identification with Christ helps the priest to overcome any stiffness and imbues him with the Lord's kindness, his loving understanding and his desire to communicate with his brethren in a very familiar way.

The priest's own faith imparts itself to the eucharistic community and leads to another important experience: all become aware that they are the community of Christ, the family of God's beloved children, and they experience true brotherhood. Only in the light of this twofold experience—their encounter with Christ and their reunion as brothers under his guidance— will it be possible to evaluate the importance of the active participation of the whole assembly and its dialogue with the priest. Whatever hinders a deep experience of Christ's presence within his community and of their brotherhood in Christ hinders also an authentic celebration and consequently the community commitment to a truly Christian life.

Let us take as an example the music used in the eucharistic celebration. Songs and musical instruments certainly can help very much in letting us experience our togetherness and in evoking the sentiments that should characterize our celebration. Music contributes especially in providing a religious atmosphere. But that does not mean that any kind of music can help us to experience union with Christ. The criterion for the proper selection of songs and instruments must be that they will help to create such a genuinely religious atmosphere in this particular community during this particular service.

It would take a special study to show more in detail how all parts of the Eucharist are to be coordinated in such a way that they can contribute effectively to the experiences of Christ's presence and of Christian brotherhood. Here we will have to limit ourselves to a few points of special importance.

The entrance rites can be of great help in giving the whole celebration from its beginning the character of Christ's encounter with his community. The way the priest enters the congregation which is already assembled; the way the participants greet Christ in his priest and at the same time express their own mutual union and desire to praise God together with Christ; the first words with which the priest greets the people in the name of Christ, inviting them to serious reflection on their Christian life as a preparation for the renewal and deepening of their commitment—all of these contribute to the religious atmosphere. It should not be one of fearful awe but rather one of deep reverence and filial confidence, of brotherly love and of personal union with Christ.

The participants thus can be aware from the first moments of the celebration that Christ is in the midst of his community: he teaches them; he prays and acts with them. The celebration, of course, will differ according to the particular circumstances: for example, a solemn celebration of the Eucharist on a great feast day in which thousands participate without knowing one another, or the familiar celebration of a small and homogeneous group. Nonetheless, in both cases the entrance rite is of great importance in setting the atmosphere. In both cases we have to avoid any kind of routine or irreverence; we have to try to create an atmosphere of joy, reverential familiarity and reflection.

In the liturgy of the word, the community should listen with true spiritual hunger to the word of God and accept it as guidance for their life here and now. Christ speaks again to his brethren—pointing out the way they are to take, challenging them to a Christian life consistent with their particular situation, consoling them in their trials and frustrations, answering their pressing problems, animating them to an ever more generous dedication without any compromise with the prince of this world. In order for the liturgy of the word to fulfill its function, the priest then helps in a very special way with his homily.

What Makes the Homily a Genuine Evangelization?

If the homily is really to be a genuine evangelization, one must be aware above all of the special catechetical objective of a good homily and its function within the eucharistic celebration. The homily must be viewed as a true catechesis because the homily, more than any other catechetical activity, has to "lead both the communities and individual members of the faithful to maturity of faith" (General Catechetical Directory, no. 21).

In the measure that the catechist leads his audience to mature faith, helping them really to understand the main concern of God's saving plan and to accept it as the meaning of their lives, he truly evangelizes them. How then is it possible that so many Christians of good will who have already heard countless homilies still manifest such immature faith?

The catechetical genre of the homily is determined by its relation to the eucharistic celebration. Within this celebration it has a threefold function. First and foremost, it has to offer the necessary help for proper understanding of the Scripture selections. Christians who lack theological formation often have considerable difficulty in grasping the meaning of the readings in the liturgy of the word.

In most cases there is not sufficient time for a thorough explanation of the texts. Very often it is not easy (and also not necessary) to show the logical coherence of the various selections. What counts much more is that the homilist explain some important point in the texts so that his listeners will understand their Christian religion more clearly and will live it more enthusiastically in their daily lives.

The word of God is never a message proclaimed in a vacuum; it always proclaims the love of God to a particular congregation and challenges it to a particular response. The most important question in preparing the homily should be: What does God intend with these texts, or at least on the occasion of these texts, to tell us here and now in our particular situation?

Like any catechetical instruction, the readings never have in view merely some interesting information; they are always meant to provide a message of life, an invitation to a new life better and more committed than until now. Without the help of the homilist the better part of the congregation cannot benefit from the full fruit of God's word. A good homily really "serves" the word of God and leads to an ever deeper appreciation of Scripture. In our homilies we should often encourage the faithful to read the Bible privately and give them the necessary directives for their private reading.

Further, the homily prepares the assembled community for the following Eucharist. For this celebration of thanksgiving, we best prepare ourselves by reflection upon the benefits that we want to acknowledge. It is especially this "eucharistic" function in the strict sense of the word that makes a good homily genuine evangelization.

It is true that in any authentic catechesis we present the joyful tidings of God's love, for the saving love of God is the main message of all Christian preaching and catechesis worthy of its name. Yet the homily that has the task of preparing for the joyful celebration of God's "marvels" puts a special emphasis on this characteristic aspect of Christian revelation. In a good homily we not only explain the particular topic in the light of God's love, but we often show its inner connection with the celebration that follows. Provided that we do not lose ourselves in peripheral themes but concentrate on the fundamental doctrines of our faith, it will always be easy to show a connection between the theme and the Eucharist which by its very nature proclaims and applies the work of redemption.

All of this is not to imply that homilies should not mention doctrines like sin, repentance or even the just punishment that the sinner brings upon himself by his rejection of God's love. Yet all of these truths receive a new look when we present them in the light of the love which the heavenly Father in this hour of grace offers to us once again through his Son. No other form of catechesis is by its nature so much a proclamation of God's love as the catechesis by which we prepare our brothers for the joyful celebration of the mysteries of that love.

Finally, the homily is supposed to dispose the community for the renewal of their Christian commitment. In each Eucharist we acknowledge again and with great joy God's goodness and respond to it with our commitment of love and filial service. This is the "prophetic" dimension of any good homily. In fulfilling his prophetic task, the "prophet" should never use his precious time for severe lectures against those absent, but rather try to influence those present to live the Gospel according to their particular situation.

Pastors who for so long have neglected a true evangelization should not expect from their faithful an immediate and thorough conversion. The evangelization given by good homilies is more like a moderate but continuing rain that is far more effective than an occasional cloudburst. Brief daily homilies are a great help. Until now we have made far too little use of the pastoral opportunities available at weekday Masses to form a nucleus of fully committed Christians.

In any true catechesis, the catechist acts as a spokesman for Christ. In the catechesis during the Eucharist, this is especially true. The celebrating priest represents Christ in a most special way. It is through him that Christ addresses his brethren and prepares them for the Eucharist to follow, implying a new and more committed acceptance of the Gospel.

What else, after all, is the Eucharist if not our ratification of the new covenant which Christ concluded on Calvary and which is ratified and renewed by us in each Eucharist? With the homily, Christ prepares his community for their commitment to live his life in the world today. Without this commitment, the Eucharist would be an empty ceremony.

After what we have said about the aim of a homily and its function within the eucharistic celebration, the following questions may prove helpful in preparing a homily with really evangelizing power:

1. What is the message Christ wants to convey through these readings to this particular community? Sometimes it may be better to first ask oneself: What is the important message Christ wants to convey to this community today? Then select readings according to the topic being treated. Remember that changes in the Sunday readings are not permitted without a grave reason.

2. What is the connection of the particular topic with the

center of the Christian message, that is, with the Gospel of God's love?

3. What does this message mean for the life of this community?

4. What is the inner connection of this theme and the eucharistic celebration?

The integration of the homily into the prayer-action of the Eucharist makes it, of course, more forceful. Here we meet a basic principle of any true evangelization that does not often receive sufficient stress. True evangelization needs an atmosphere of prayer. It originates from an attitude of prayer.

The message of the Gospel is never primarily the product of human speculation and planning. The "evangelist" receives it first in an atmosphere of prayer. In an atmosphere of union with God he has to transmit it to others. Only in an atmosphere of prayer can it produce real fruit. "I planted the seed, Apollos watered the plant, but it was God who made the plant grow" (1 Cor. 3:6).

A good homily does not need to be long. Provided that those who take part in the Eucharist are truly evangelized, the homily should be rather short. However, it must always be warm, substantial, and carefully adapted to the particular congregation and its spiritual needs.

There is, nevertheless, a special problem involved with regard to Sunday Mass homilies that deserves careful attention. We speak a great deal today about the pressing need of adult catechesis, and we are right to stress this need. Any realistic evaluation of the opportunities available for such evangelization indicates that the homily at Sunday Mass is our best medium for reaching these adult Catholics and forming them.

Many Christians have a most superficial knowledge of their religion, and in the present era of doctrinal vagueness and confusion they are exposed to serious dangers to their faith. Daily they face the powerful influence of a secularized world with its alluring vision of life without God. Our mass media and all the avenues of advertising show us a world in which God and the norms of real Christian living count for very little.

In such circumstances can we realistically hope with short

homilies of seven to ten minutes to give our brothers and sisters the clear, well-founded orientation they need for an authentic Christian life in this "post-Christian" world? It may be that we cannot extend the time assigned to the homily at all Sunday Masses. But what deters us from longer homilies at least in some Masses, as well as celebrating these Masses with a homily that is especially well prepared and with a celebration clearly superior to the shorter Masses?

Chapter Eight
Human Development and Liberation in Evangelization

The Gospel message is the Good News of salvation. Evangelization proclaims the salvation that God has promised and that he imparts to all who accept his message. All Christians admit this. But what is the real meaning of this salvation which we proclaim in the name of God?

The Problem

Salvation must involve the well-being of those who are to be saved. That said, we must ask further: What is meant by this well-being that is promised and sought. Very different answers can be given to this question.

In times past, salvation was commonly understood in the eschatological sense. The answer was clear and simple. Salvation, we were told, meant that we should prepare ourselves in this world to be worthy to enjoy a later life in the Kingdom of God. We should, of course, assume that the gift of God's life was ours in this life as something great and real. God has already made us his sons. Even now in this "valley of tears," he shares his own life with us; he consoles us and visits us with profound spiritual joys.

But, in such an answer, it was presumed that God expected us to leave insofar as possible our preoccupation with this transitory world and its development and its enjoyment to the "children of the world": "Brothers, this is what I mean: our time is growing short. . . . Those whose life is buying things should live as though they had nothing of their own; and those who have to deal with the world should not become engrossed in it. I say this because the world as we know it is passing away" (1 Cor. 7:29-31).

Who can deny that many texts of Scripture seem to require such an attitude. Another typical text asserts: "Since you have been brought back to life with Christ, you must look for the things that are in heaven where Christ is seated at God's right hand. Let your thoughts be upon heavenly things, not on the things that are on the earth, because you have died and now the life you have is hidden with Christ in God. But when Christ is revealed   and he is your life—you too will be revealed in all your glory with him" (Col. 3:1-4). From among many passages (see, e.g., Mt. 5:25-34; Lk. 9:24; 12:32-34; Phil. 3:20f; Heb. 11:13; 1 Pet. 2:11) we have chosen this Pauline text, since it is particularly specific in its connection with the center of the Christian message.

There can be no possible doubt that in the early Church salvation was proclaimed with great emphasis upon its eschatological aspect. From the beginning of Christianity, and throughout the whole Christian era, many "evangelists" gave little attention to the temporal values of human life. On the one hand, man because of his spiritual blindness and his inordinate desire for earthly goods needed special emphasis placed on spiritual values. On the other hand, the lack of good balance has provoked in our own times undue insistence on earthly values, and this tends to adulterate the Christian message.

Under the influence of modern secularism and of Marxist philosophy, we encounter diverse efforts to secularize the salvation of man and to interpret this as a form of human development. People who want to remain Christians do not deny the spiritual; they still admit the existence of another life to come. But the practical emphasis is clearly laid on temporal values. What is proclaimed primarily is a Gospel of temporal development.

The last Synod of Bishops declared itself clearly opposed to this secularization of the Christian message. Yet the Synod, as well as Vatican II, recognized that merely condemning this secularized interpretation of salvation would not solve the problem. What is needed is a balanced response which on the one hand does justice to the Gospel, and, on the other, takes into account the relation of men today to the world around them.

In the light of faith, we Christians consider our temporal existence as a preparation for something greater and definitive, something that will bring us final fulfillment. Yet this does not oblige us to deny the value of the world that God created for us and the material goods available.

Let us consider a comparison. Two fathers want to test the love and obedience of their sons, but they do it in very different ways. The first father orders his sons to do something meaningless, for example, to run up and down the stairs of their home fifty-three times each day. The second father asks his sons to lend a hand in making their home more comfortable and beautiful so that they can enjoy life there even more. Which of these fathers uses the right method? Which of them imitates our heavenly Father in testing the obedience of his sons?

In times past, theology and catechesis did not explain with sufficient clarity the function and value of the temporal order in God's plan of salvation. The Council therefore insisted upon this point in a special way: "Many elements make up the temporal order: namely, the good things of life and the prosperity of the family, culture, economic affairs, the arts and professions, political institutions, international relations and other mattes of this kind, as well as their development and progress. All of these not only aid in the attainment of man's ultimate goal, but also possess their own intrinsic value" (*Decree on the Apostolate of the Laity*, no. 7).

This and similar tenets of the Council (see especially the *Constitution on the Church in the Modern World*, no. 42), which are based on the word of God, declare emphatically the essential goodness of the temporal order. The temporal goods are not just means for attaining final happiness, but rather have their own value. And what is even more important for man, the plan of salvation demands that he must prove his acceptance of God's saving love by a serious commitment to contribute selflessly to the betterment of this world. He who is not ready to work diligently and consistently in the temporal garden of the Father proves himself unfit for the heavenly mansions.

Pope Paul has defined the consequences of all this for authentic evangelization in his allocution at the beginning of the last Synod of Bishops. "Missionaries of today," the Holy Father said, "are in danger when they forget the priority due to the message of salvation and in this way reduce their work to mere socio-political activity and reduce the message of Christ to a man-centered and temporal one. This, however, does not mean that in evangelization one could or should ignore the importance of the problems, so much discussed today, concerning justice, liberation, development and peace in the world" (*Osservatore Romano*, Oct. 10, 1974, p. 10).

Thus the pope declared explicitly that these important themes are not to be neglected and that they must be correctly integrated into the Christian message. Within that message, they have an important place, although an essentially subordinate one. Surely it is not enough to admit that "on principle" the religious aspect deserves priority but in fact to neglect this priority and turn the Gospel into a message essentially humanistic and temporal.

The concern of evangelization for the temporal order today is usually grouped under two headings: human development and liberation.

Human Development

The first pages of the Bible provide us with the basic principle regarding man's place and task in this world. In metaphorical language which aptly uses mythical elements of ancient cultures, the Bible presents a fundamental message. Man is the masterpiece of God. He is not only the most perfect creature in this visible world; God has solemnly installed him as master of the world, yet definitely under the supremacy of God. With unmistakable emphasis, man is told to master and subdue the world and everything he finds in it, and to make use of all for his own purposes (see Gen. 1:26-28). The entire world is

God's gift to man by which God proves his love from the very beginning. The loving intention of God is obvious: he loves man and desires his well-being in this world.

Man needs the experience of God's love in his earthly life. Without this experience how could man become convinced of God's love and desire union with him forever? Throughout the Scriptures, man's temporal life and all the goods he needs to maintain, develop and enjoy it are portrayed as precious gifts of God. However, man must acknowledge God as the ultimate gift and be grateful to him.

How does God give to man everything he needs for his well-being here on earth? It is significant that God from the beginning placed man in a garden and ordered him, even before the first sin, "to cultivate and take care of it" (Gen. 2:15). The temporal goods do not fall down from heaven. They did not do so in paradise; man wins them only by his diligent collaboration with God's plan of creation.

True, man can anticipate these goods with filial confidence in God's bounty (see Mt. 6:30), but he must never do this with slothful confidence. Even expectation of the imminent coming of the Lord in glory cannot justify such indolent confidence. St. Paul retorts: "Whoever does not want to work is not allowed to eat" (2 Thes. 3:10; see also Prv. 6:6-10).

It is not even enough to work to maintain one's own life. True Christians must "try to find some useful manual work and be able to do some good by helping others who are in need" (Eph. 4:28). Whoever does not dedicate himself resolutely to the well-being of his neighbor runs the risk of losing his eternal salvation (see Mt. 25:41-46). In describing the Last Judgment, Christ speaks directly only of the promotion of the temporal well-being of man.

In the solemn proclamation of the new life according to the Gospel, which we find in the Sermon on the Mount (Mt. 5—7; Lk. 6:17-49), Jesus on the one hand asks his disciples for perfect interior freedom regarding temporal goods, and, on the other, for a dedication to the well-being of neighbor that calls even for heroic sacrifices. And this is demanded not just occasionally but as a basic permanent attitude: "So always treat others as you would like them to treat you; that is the meaning of the law and the prophets" (Mt. 7:12).

Such a gift of self is a necessary consequence of the fundamental law of Christianity—the law of love. We are Christians to the extent that we love God with our whole heart and prove our love by our sincere interest in the total well-being of our neighbor. "Anyone who says 'I love God' and hates his brothers is a liar, since a man who does not love the brother that he can see cannot love God whom he has never seen" (1 Jn. 4:20).

At the same time, these texts prove how profoundly interested God is in the complete well-being of man. The salvation of man consists, according to the plan of God, not only in man's final happiness but in the promotion and attainment of his complete well-being, yet always with the necessary subordination of the temporal according to its place in the whole.

The fact that the heart is more important than the foot surely does not mean that we may disregard the foot or even cut it off, but it does mean that a preoccupation with the well-being of the foot that disregards the heart is even more unpardonable. In an extreme case, a foot may be sacrificed in order to save the heart, but the heart can never be sacrificed in order to save the foot.

Through the Gospel, God challenges us to a devout collaboration with him for the complete well-being of man as an individual person and for the well-being of the human community excluding no one. This complete well-being obviously involves much more than economic prosperity with an abundance of material goods and a dearth of the higher values of human culture. The progress of culture implies a supply of basic material goods, but it places the greater emphasis on these values which recognize and support man as an intelligent, free and social body-person.

Divine revelation does not tell us in particular how the total prosperity of man can be achieved, nor does it tell us what deserves priority in a given situation or which methods would be the most efficient. Man himself must find that out through his own research and study.

God did not reveal to us these specifics, and therefore, the Church has no authority to make binding decisions in this regard (see the *Constitution on the Church in the Modern World*, no. 36). Such decisions also do not belong to the content of evangelization. What the Church must faithfully proclaim in her evangelization, without any cowardly compromise, are the basic principles of man's dignity as a free person, of social justice and of peace. To expect the Church to interfere in particular cases and pronounce authoritatively on them would lead us back to the false ecclesial theocracy of the Middle Ages.

Under the influence of modern science with its insistence upon the evolution of the whole universe, we have gained new and profound insights into God's plan of creation and salvation. To Christians, evolution means much more than a blind tendency to ever greater perfection observable as an elementary force underlying the whole universe. Rather, evolution manifests to us a special aspect of God's plan of creation.

With the exception of man, all creatures of the universe blindly follow the laws of evolution. According to their nature, they each contribute to the betterment of the world. Only man is the free co-worker of God. God challenges him to make a personal contribution to the achievement of the divine plan. As we now know from science, man did not come into existence as a fully developed being. At the beginning he was still very primitive.

According to God's plan, man must prove his obedience to God by continuous and vigorous efforts to overcome his primitiveness; he must actualize his tremendous potential in a life and culture that expresses ever more perfectly his human dignity. Human development, therefore, is the "yes" of man to the plan of creation. The Christian commits himself to carry out this plan with ever increasing effort, ever increasing perfection. At the same time, he remains aware that any temporal existence, no matter how much better than his present one, will still be only a limited anticipation of the world of resurrection.

In recent years, especially in the Third World, many protagonists of human development have become heralds of human liberation. It is worthwhile to consider the aspect of liberation separately and to see its connection with the salvation of man.

Liberation

The present heralds of liberation usually admit that by this word they mean, to a great extent, human development, but they insist that "liberation" is more suited to the current situation, especially in Latin America and other parts of the Third World.

The main exponent of this trend of thought is Gustavo Gutiérrez with his book *A Theology of Liberation* (Maryknoll, N.Y., 1973). The term "human development," we are told, is used too exclusively to describe material progress, which, in fact, leads to the further enrichment of the upper class of human society and the further impoverishment of the others. And it is true that because of the disproportionate influence of the rich and powerful upon the mass media and in public life, human development has often been misunderstood and propagated in this erroneous and harmful sense.

Obviously such selfish progress for one class of human society to the detriment of others contradicts the Gospel. But like the term "human development," "liberation" is also in danger of being misunderstood. In fact, it is often understood in the sense of propagating licentiousness, again in contradiction to the Gospel. Of course, the fact that a word is misunderstood and abused does not imply an obligation to avoid it; it only implies the duty to use it carefully and with the necessary explanation.

Many writers today understand liberation primarily in terms of political and economic liberation and give the impression that social and political liberation is the most pressing need. Sometimes this is done to the extent that the Gospel of love becomes mere propaganda for social revolution. Thus the term "liberation" also needs to be used with discretion.

Such abuses, however, should not let us overlook the fact that liberation stresses important aspects of creation and salvation as they have been planned by God. It is definitely worthwhile, therefore, to reflect upon the place of liberation in presenting the Christian message. Whereas human development is not a biblical term, liberation surely is, although it is now often used in a way different than in Scripture.

The term "liberation" can be used in two ways, and both usages have their legitimate place in the proclamation of the Gospel. In one sense, liberation can be understood as rescuing man from all the obstacles that hinder his true well-being, and especially from everything that hinders the development and use of his freedom. If salvation consists in the total well-being of man, rescuing him from all obstacles to it obviously constitutes an essential part of that salvation.

Such liberation, it is true, does not yet mean a positive direct increase in his well-being; it simply removes the hindrances. But as man really is and in this world always will be, this "negative" contribution is extremely important. A sincere interest in the well-being of individual men and of the entire community requires, of course, massive efforts to remove those hindrances.

The protagonists of liberation describe the hindrances well. They are many and great. There is an acute danger that many Christians, because of their self-centered attitude, do not recognize them. Such Christians recite in vain the last petition of the Our Father. Just as those who are not willing to forgive others are not themselves forgiven, so, too, those who are not willing to deliver others from evil will not themselves be delivered.

The heralds of liberation are also right when they insist on the dreadful consequences of misery, oppression, injustice and corruption as all too often encountered in today's world. Even worse than the resulting physical suffering are the moral evils to which they lead. They hinder especially the experience of personal dignity; they enslave the man who is disregarded and oppressed; they block the development of the individual and the community.

It is also true that the official heralds of the Gospel have not always denounced these evils as the Gospel obliges them to do; even worse, quite a few have allied themselves with persons in power who caused these evils. Yes, it was necessary to appeal to the sleeping consciences of these unfaithful "evangelists." Yet this does not justify exaggerations from the other side.

An especially difficult and delicate problem consists in the force and, in extreme cases, the violence which is said to be necessary to combat the undeniable obstinacy and violence of the oppressors in power. We must admit the existence of the situations which caused this problem, but even in such an extreme case we are never allowed to give the impression that the Gospel is primarily a socio-political message, nor are we permitted to disregard the fundamental attitude of Christian love that must also include enemies. A Gospel of hate is not the Gospel of Christ.

The true herald of the Gospel must always insist upon mutual understanding. He must always favor fair and realistic solutions; he must strive to equalize the contrasts and ease the tensions. He must always try to unite those at variance in sincere common prayer, for he believes in the wonderful power of truly Christian prayer. It cannot always solve the problems but it helps to bridge them. A messenger of the Gospel who identifies himself blindly with one side cannot expect that the other will accept his message.

The second usage of the term "liberation" is thoroughly positive and means the improvement of human freedom. Here we are no longer speaking of the obstacles that man encounters in his life situation; rather, we speak of the gradual improvement of man's freedom from within. This improvement, however, depends tremendously on the conditions each man encounters in his daily life.

In the past the "freedom of man" has been looked upon as a power innate within the very nature of man. We readily forget that primitive man was much more under the power of his instinctive impulses than is today's educated man, and also that each individual man must grow in an ever increasing control of his impulses as he strives toward true freedom.

Perfect freedom is also at times interpreted as a state in which man is in a position to follow his own caprices without any controls from without or orientations from within to pilot him toward a particular direction or goal. Such interpreters never seem to remember that such a state is exactly what the Bible condemns as un-Christian licentiousness (see, e.g., Gal. 5:13; 2 Pet. 2:19).

Some men have never really understood that the true freedom which Christ brought to us as a gift of salvation means something much greater—the possibility for mature man to evaluate correctly the objects which present themselves for his choice and the readiness to decide without harmful disturbance from without or within which is the most worthy.

What impedes us from giving ourselves readily and generously to God who deserves our wholehearted commitment is precisely our own selfishness. True freedom, therefore, frees us from ourselves. How few Christians consider as the highway to authentic freedom the word of our Lord: "For anyone who saves his life will lose it, but anyone who loses his life for my sake will find it" (Mt. 16:25). This fundamental directive of our Lord we find, significantly, in all four Gospels in almost the same formulation (see also Mk. 8:35; Lk. 9:24; Jn. 12:24).

The Lord himself stresses the close connection of this perfect freedom with the gift of salvation. The abuse of freedom enslaves us; we become "slaves of sin" (cf. Jn. 8:34; Rom. 6:17; 6:20). True and perfect freedom which is a gift from God makes us servants of God (see 1 Pet. 2:16), not forced servants but servants out of love. Such theological deepening of the meaning of true liberation is very definitely a valuable contribution to the understanding of the Gospel. But can we sincerely say today that human liberation is usually presented with the necessary theological precision and depth?

In the last Synod the bishops did not really come to terms with the question of how the themes of human development and liberation relate to the Gospel. All agreed that these themes have an important place within the Christian message and must, therefore, be considered at least integral parts of it, but there was no consensus as to whether they could be considered even as constitutive elements belonging to the very substance of the Good News.

Sincere and deep concern for the total well-being of one's neighbor is undoubtedly a constitutive element of the Gospel clearly spelled out as such by the Lord himself in the central command of Christianity (cf. Mt. 22:39f). Yet this concern for one's neighbor must be seen in the light of our relationship to God. Its application and formulation may vary tremendously according to particular situations. And even if we acknowledge the themes of human development and liberation as constitutive elements, we are still not dispensed in any way from the responsibility for integrating them properly into the whole of the Christian message.

Chapter Nine
The Evangelist

"At various times in the past and in various ways, God spoke to our ancestors through the prophets; but in our own time, the last days, he has spoken to us through his Son" (Heb. 1:1f). "Go out to the whole world; proclaim the Good News to all creation. He who believes and is baptized will be saved; he who does not believe will be condemned" (Mk. 16:15f). "The footsteps of those who bring good news is a welcome sound" (Rom. 10:15).

The joyful message of salvation is the gift of the loving Father, but this message of life and love reaches man through men who are sent by God. No one receives the Good News and grows in the life of faith without the mediation of men. Very few find God only through books, which again, after all, include human instrumentality.

For our journey to God, for the first acceptance of the Gospel and for the growth of faith that follows, personal encounters are usually of much greater importance than books.

By "evangelist," we here mean the person who acts as God's instrument in transmitting the good news of salvation to others. Thus the questions arise: Who are the ones who have the privilege and at the same time the obligation to serve God as heralds of his Gospel, and what are the characteristics and, more important, the qualities of the true evangelist?

Who Has the Privilege and Duty
of Evangelizing Others?

First of all, we have to insist upon a fundamental principle

102

which, unfortunately, is often forgotten or, at least, not taken seriously. All those who have correctly understood and sincerely accepted the Gospel of Christ have the privilege and obligation of radiating their new life to those around them. A life according to the Gospel which one keeps for himself without any desire to share it with others is a contradiction in terms. No one receives the pearl of the Gospel just for himself.

There are many Christians who rarely think of their own salvation; they preoccupy themselves even less with the salvation of others. To such people, the Christian life is an inevitable obligation and not a joyful experience. They listen with one ear only to the invitation of the Lord. Such an attitude, of course, hardly inspires one to proclaim the Good News.

But how is it possible that so many Christians of good will keep the divine treasure to themselves without being aware of their un-Christian attitude. Usually these people consider faith to be a private affair meant for their own spiritual enrichment and orientation of life, not for dialogue and sharing with others.

There are also many unhappy Christians who live a sad religious life and in consequence make the faith very unappealing to others. In spite of their good will, they have never become aware of the essentially joyful character of the Christian religion. These poor people have never really been evangelized and therefore are unable to evangelize others.

What we are trying to stress here is simply this: the Gospel by its very nature is good tidings. It must be transmitted as such to others and is intended to lead to deep communicative joy whenever it is received with a sincere heart. Those who receive the Gospel must experience a challenge to communicate this Good News which sets man free and brings him fulfillment.

The same holds true for any authentic spiritual direction. Spiritual direction that does not form evangelists does not form real Christians; it fosters, instead, a sad and depressed attitude or, at least, a false sense of contentment.

What counts most here is the foundation and systematic furtherance of an evangelistic mentality, but there is also a need to suggest concrete possibilities of passing on the Good News to others. There are numerous and manifold opportunities for this in the life of every Christian. In the next chapter, which deals with various opportunities for evangelization, this point will be developed further.

All who have been evangelized are called to evangelize others, but not all are called to make the same contribution, nor are all called to the same degree. The measure available to each Christian depends upon his particular life-situation and also his individual character and talents.

No one, however, can dispense himself from this obligation to make his own contribution, either because of a seeming lack of talents or because of a lack of responsibility for others. The fact that some people have a special duty to evangelize growing out of their particular vocation, as is the case with parents, catechists and priests, does not permit others to be satisfied with a self-centered life devoid of any serious efforts to share the faith.

Among those who are called to communicate and witness their faith, parents have a place of special importance. As Christians, they have the great privilege and fundamental task of inspiring their children from the years of infancy with the Gospel of God's love. The way in which the Christian religion is shared and lived in a family is in the majority of cases the deciding factor in one's religious attitude throughout adult life.

From indifferent families come forth Christians without any interest in religion; from families with a legalistic and ritualistic approach, we can only expect legalists and ritualists with little personal experience of God and his love. Families with a religion of fear can only produce Christians whose God is a caricature of a Father, an inexorable judge who requires much and gives little—a tyrant who does not deserve and does not receive love.

Christian *parents*, mothers and fathers alike, must take account of their vocation as messengers of the Gospel and must accept and fulfill it wholeheartedly. Since God has revealed himself to us as our loving Father, fathers hold a very special place in the religious education of their families. The best mother evangelizes in vain if the father does not help as he should, or if the father does not give a favorable father image so necessary to help the children ascend from the earthly father to the Father of all things from whom every perfect gift comes (Jas. 1:17).

More than in any other form of evangelization, the whole atmosphere of home and life must be a major factor in family evangelization. Parents who cannot create a truly Christian atmosphere in the home are poor evangelists. Not infrequently, parents show interest in Christian education for their children simply to make them more manageable and submissive. Such education does not evangelize but enslaves, and the consequences are disastrous. Especially today, children are quick to detect any selfish intention of their parents. They will be angered by their parents' scheme and during adolescence they will reject the God who was given the role of taming them.

Priests, of course, are evangelists of great importance. Their ordination not only gives them sacred powers regarding the sacraments but demands of them a special share in the prophetic office of Jesus Christ. In other words, priests are ordained for the total service they must give, in close union with Christ, the High Priest and perfect Servant, to the Christian community through the proclamation of the Gospel, the administration of the sacraments and pastoral care.

Priests are prepared through extensive theological studies to proclaim the word as well as possible. Yet the special quality of priestly evangelization ultimately depends on something more. The evangelical-sacramental ordination is by its very nature a consecration. The priest must respond by presenting the principal elements of the Gospel message with great insight, great depth and clarity, and great reverence. More doctrinal precision and orthodoxy are not enough. The priest who is worthy of his priesthood will be eager to proclaim the Gospel. In his evangelic zeal he will seek out opportunities to proclaim it, especially to those most in need.

Priestly evangelization must also be marked by its correct integration into the whole of priestly activities. The priest must avoid all faulty sacramentalism that puts the emphasis upon routine administration of the sacraments without solid evangelization as the necessary preparation for their proper reception. Since priests are the God-given leaders in the work of evangelization, any neglect here on the part of pastors will almost always result in a low standard of evangelization throughout the domain entrusted to their care. A priest may rightly consider his sacramental activity as the most noble part of his work but his main efforts must be made in the area of evangelization. Is that not, after all, what we learn from Christ and his apostles?

Such emphasis on priestly evangelization does not, of course, mean that the priest should ever try to consider evangelization his monopoly. He must train others for this work; he must inspire them, guide them and work together with them in the true spirit of collegiality. This will require his own sincere appreciation of evangelization and his constant dedication to the work. Bishops, too, as successors of the apostles, have a serious obligation to dedicate their main efforts to the proper proclamation of the Gospel. The popes of the last century were outstanding in this regard.

The great bulk of catechetical work in parishes and Christian schools is done by *religion teachers*—religious and lay. The Church is deeply indebted to them for their dedication to this important and difficult work.

The value of such catechetical activity depends essentially upon the truly evangelizing character of their catechesis. In the selection of prospective catechists, the chief criteria must be that they are willing to become, and are capable of becoming, authentic evangelists. And the entire formation given to prepare them for this apostolate must be aimed principally at making them true messengers of the Gospel. This necessarily implies that special care will be given to the strictly spiritual aspect of their training, leading them to a correct and deeply religious understanding of the Gospel message they will be proclaiming. This, of course, will not minimize the other aspects of their training, but it does require that priorities be carefully set. Who would deny that such formation has often been neglected in the past? Not much can be expected from a salesman who does not really know his product and is not personally interested in what he is offering, even if he is a master of advertising.

The obligation to evangelize rests not only with individual Christians but also with the *Christian community*. Like all

Christian life, so too the work of evangelization in recent centuries has often been regarded in too individualistic a manner. Modern catechetics correctly stresses the great and often decisive role of the community in evangelization. The General Catechetical Directory aptly expresses this new trend when it says: "In catechesis, the importance of the group is becoming greater and greater. . . . For adolescents and adults, the group must be considered a vital necessity. . . . In the case of adults, the group can today be considered as a requisite for catechesis which aims at fostering a sense of Christian co-responsibility" (no. 76).

The tremendous formative power of family catechesis, for example, rests on the fact that it is not an individual—however highly respected he may be, such as the father or mother—but the entire group that evangelizes, and this not with school lectures but through the intimate daily living of persons who matter most to one another. We add in this connection that a truly Christian family life evangelizes not only the children but also the parents.

The reasons why the community has great evangelizing power are obvious. The community with its experience of life is usually much more convincing than an individual who can offer only his personal witness and conviction. The Gospel message challenges us to a new life. The individual evangelist can describe this life attractively; he can stimulate us by his own example. But he usually does not remain with us, does not live with us.

The community surrounds us, molds us, convinces us of the possibility and the existential value of a truly Christian life. Evangelizing catechesis must lead to a genuine experience of God's presence in our lives. With the exception of extraordinary encounters with God that include mystical elements, we never experience his presence so deeply in this life as we do within a community which is thoroughly committed to a Christian life without compromise.

With the community's life of prayer and mutual love, we experience—in a joyful and convincing manner—God's presence in the midst of his people. With the aid of God's grace, an individual evangelist can lead one to a change of life, a true conversion. The community welcomes the converted brother and facilitates his perseverance and progress in the Christian life. Its members go with him on the same journey to God and share with him the same life-experiences.

Of course, the community as such cannot work these wonders of evangelization. As in the case of an individual evangelist, everything here again depends on the *quality* of the community that evangelizes and ultimately on God as the source of its power. A community that does not truly live the Christian life is a great obstacle to evangelization. And it is generally conceded that many individual communities within the institutional Church today are more of a hindrance than a help.

In order to evaluate correctly the evangelizing power of a particular community, we must remember that its evangelizing effficiency is not due to its juridical character but primarily to the depth and genuineness of its community life. Intensive and outstanding community life cannot be actualized in large communities. It is essential to break them up into small dynamic groups to guarantee true sharing. This is the main reason why efficacious evangelization of big parishes can only be expected from small groups which are formed within the larger community and then revitalize it.

The Main Qualities of a True Evangelist

The office someone holds within the Church may involve a special obligation to evangelize. It may also require a special type of evangelization, but it does not by itself confer upon him or her the qualities of a good evangelist, nor do the natural gifts or God's grace, though surely important, produce worthy evangelists. Also necessary is the free and diligent collaboration of the one who receives these gifts.

What is commonly called the "grace of office" is not a replacement for the indispensable efforts of the officeholder. The one who desires to evangelize well must make the necessary efforts to develop in himself the qualities of a good evangelist, and the qualities he needs can be learned through some simple reflection on the nature of evangelization.

The evangelist transmits the message that he himself has received. This requires *great fidelity* on his part. He must present not his own opinions or theories but the word of God without any additions of his own, neither omitting any necessary elements nor disfiguring in any way the message entrusted to him. He must stress only what God stresses in his revelation, and that is, above all, God's loving concern for man.

Here we meet with an intricate problem that can never be solved completely, although it requires a solution that is as adequate as possible. On the one hand, the Gospel cannot be transmitted mechanically as one passes on a piece of wood to someone else. The Gospel message must be assimilated by the evangelist himself. He must make it truly his own before he can transmit it to others in a personal manner. In this transmission he must also adapt himself to those whom he is evangelizing. He must proclaim the perennial Gospel message in their language, in their categories of thought and according to their particular life situation. This requires an assimilation and adaptation which far surpasses any mere adaptation of the language. If seen in its most profound dimensions, it is essentially more than mere adaptation. The Gospel definitely challenges men to make it their own, to express it in their own way of thinking and lifestyle.

On the other hand, fidelity obliges the evangelist to transmit the Gospel in its full purity and not as an inextricable mixture of divine and human elements. A satisfactory solution to this very real problem can only be achieved by an evangelist who is at the same time outstanding both for his fidelity and for his prayerful reflection. Such reflection helps him to understand the true intention of God's revelation and the peculiarities of those who are called by God. Prayerful reflection also helps him to understand that God is not interested in dead formulas but only in personal communication with men. And such communication always requires the personal contribution of the one who accepts, assimilates and transmits the Gospel.

At the same time, the evangelist's fidelity disposes him to strive sincerely to understand correctly the word of God, to accept it wholeheartedly and to transmit it without alteration. This fidelity prods the evangelist to diligent and careful study of the Gospel. It makes him eager to mine the Gospel message from its primary sources, from the Scriptures and from the authentic doctrinal statements of the Church. A deep and practical appreciation of the Scriptures leading to biblical spirituality is one of the characteristics of a genuine evangelist. By listening attentively to God who speaks to him in Scripture, the evangelist best prepares himself to proclaim this message to his brothers and sisters.

The faithful messenger of God is well aware that he must not be satisfied with just a correct understanding of the particular doctrines. What counts even more to a certain extent is a proper understanding of the central theme of the Gospel and an appreciation of how the particular doctrines relate to that theme. The evangelist's fidelity requires him to place his primary emphasis on the key elements of the Gospel. Catechists who speak more about Fatima and St. Joseph than about the Holy Spirit seriously offend against evangelical fidelity.

Another important aspect of Gospel fidelity is the evangelist's courage. As an intrepid witness to the Good News, he must refuse all cowardly adaptation of his message, not only to the whims of those in authority but also to the fancies of those he is evangelizing. Whenever the official messenger of the Gospel lacks this courage, his evangelization loses its credibility; in the course of Christian history, there are many sad examples of this fact.

The Gospel we proclaim is by its nature a message of life, love and joy. The requisites for the life of the evangelist thus become obvious. He must, after all, evangelize more by his example than by his words. If he is not willing to do so, his master will call him a hypocrite (see Mt. 7:5; Lk. 11:46). Remember that his message is meant to challenge others to a radical reform of their lives; thus he is obliged to first reform his own. If an evangelist is lacking in such personal witness, he loses credibility; even worse, he provokes resentment against his message.

Nowadays, we rightly stress that the Gospel is, above all, a message of love. Everyone therefore expects that a messenger

announcing this love will himself be *outstanding for his love.*
Those whom he evangelizes do not see God himself; they see
only the representative of his love. The deep and selfless interest
of God's messenger in their well-being must convince these people of the love of God who has sent them this man of love.

A message of joy cannot be pronounced meaningfully by a
sad and austere messenger. If the Gospel proclaims joyful tidings, the evangelist must radiate this *evangelic joy.* What we expect from a true Gospel messenger is not a superficial and noisy
gaiety; rather, we expect a profound, permanent peace and joy
resulting from an unconditional surrender to a loving God.

Such joy is grounded not upon some fortunate natural disposition but upon unshakable faith in God's love. It is the fruit
of generous efforts to free oneself from every kind of selfishness. This liberation from oneself, to be sure, is a gift of
God's grace, but this grace is offered to every Christian of good
will on his way to God. Such true joy cannot be obtained without magnanimous self-abnegation, but it excludes every kind of
gloomy asceticism.

In times past, we obviously did not place adequate emphasis upon the fundamental importance of evangelic joy. And we
did not distinguish ourselves as we should have in forming really
joyful messengers of the Gospel.

To evangelize means to transmit the Gospel message in
such a way that those being evangelized may be helped in their
life of faith and come to an ever more mature faith. Even the
most perfect transmission of the Gospel cannot, of course, produce faith. We stressed this point in the first two chapters of this
book.

The method of transmission is, nevertheless, of capital importance in disposing others to accept the Gospel in an attitude
of faith. We must therefore insist upon *the qualities of the
evangelist which guarantee a proper transmission of the Gospel.*
A naturally communicative disposition is obviously of great
help for anyone, but in any case he needs the ability to enter
into true dialogue with others, and this can come from his natural disposition or be the result of self-training.

In today's circumstances more than ever before, we must

insist upon the willingness of the evangelist to listen to others
and to sincerely appreciate whatever is good in their thought
and life. It should, however, be remembered that evangelization
is something more than just a friendly dialogue with a lively
exchange of ideas and no commitment.

Without imposing himself in any way upon others and thus
avoiding all proselytism, the true evangelist shares with them
the riches of his own religious experience. St. Paul, the outstanding evangelist of the early Church, beautifully expressed
the characteristic attitude of a genuine messenger of the Gospel:
"I am the least of all God's people; yet God gave me this
privilege of taking to the Gentiles the Good News of the infinite
riches of Christ" (Eph. 3:8). "And this is because the love of
Christ overwhelms us" (2 Cor. 5:14).

The objective of all evangelization is mature faith in those
we evangelize. This obviously supposes *mature faith* in the evangelist himself. His whole work consists in leading others to mature faith. We have already discussed the qualities of such faith
in Chapter Two; here we will only stress that the evangelist
must be distinguished by the qualities of mature faith which he
is supposed to promote in others.

The work of evangelization is never a private enterprise.
Christ evangelizes through the instrumentality of the Church
where he is continuing his work of salvation. The individual
evangelist must see himself as a member of a team which has
Christ himself as its leader. Christ, however, makes his leadership effective through the leaders he had chosen as his delegates
within the Church. And ultimately the whole enterprise is the
work of the Holy Spirit (see Acts 20:28).

This does not, of course, mean that the work of evangelization is the monopoly of the hierarchy or of the clergy, but it
definitely means that according to God's plan the leaders have
the responsibility and the serious obligation to promote and
coordinate the entire work of evangelization within the Church.
The individual evangelist, therefore, must be ready for the
proper integration and collaboration, and this, as everybody
knows, can sometimes require great sacrifices that can only be
motivated efficaciously by deep faith.

Ecclesial superiors, bishops and pastors alike, have the serious responsibility to facilitate, animate and direct the evangelizing activity of all the faithful. They are never allowed to restrict it by their own whims or by an improper authoritarianism or centralism. At the last Synod, the bishops of Africa and other mission countries in particular demanded more freedom in their evangelization efforts.

In recent centuries, it is true, an overdose of centralism characterized the work of evangelization within the Church. Today, however, there are some signs that we are swinging to the opposite extreme. In any case, the problem will not be solved by creating more popes within the Church. It would be unfair and also wrong to consider Rome as the only source and cause of centralism. A restrictive centralism is often felt in particular dioceses, and even more in parishes with a too authoritarian pastor. To blame the wrong scapegoat is always a sign of immaturity.

Undue centralism of any kind is more liable to result in submissive and timid functionaries than in dedicated evangelists. Yet a lack of coordination and guidance endangers the success of evangelization and even the unity of the evangelic community. The question is arising as to whether the present danger of doctrinal confusion can be overcome without more guidance again being given to the ordinary evangelists who so often feel lost in today's unhealthy situation.

It is easy to describe the qualities that must distinguish a true evangelist. Acquiring them is much harder. The competent evangelist is a product of the *formation* he receives for his work and the *personal efforts* by which he appropriates, continues and deepens that formation.

When Vatican II speaks of the participation of all Christians in the apostolate, it stresses the necessity of formation and of a special formation for those who work in any type of professional apostolate (see the *Decree on the Apostolate of the Laity*, nos. 28-32). The progress of evangelization depends decisively upon such efforts to form true evangelists.

In many places this formation still leaves much to be desired, especially as regards spiritual formation. If we wish to have true messengers of the Gospel, the spiritual aspects must be given preference over all the other areas of formation. This is especially necessary because of the secularism we encounter almost everywhere today. Yet at the same time it must be clearly seen that spiritual formation has value to the extent that it is harmoniously integrated into an adequate general formation program.

Chapter Ten
Opportunities for Evangelization

A zealous evangelist will always find opportunities to spread the Good News of God's saving love. He will create such opportunities, for he feels as the apostles did when they declared: "We cannot stop speaking of what we ourselves have seen and heard" (Acts 4:20). The depth and intensity of his personal religious experience yearns for communication. A few norms given here may help in finding the most meaningful outlets for this yearning.

The Necessary Discernment of Various Opportunities

Since there are many opportunities for evangelization, judicious evaluation and discernment are needed to sort out the most fruitful. Leaders who have to plan evangelization programs and to direct other evangelists in their work must be able to discern priorities and concentrate apostolic efforts upon them. Obviously the whole world needs Christ, but what are the best ways to bring Christ to the world today?

One of the principal aims of the last Synod of Bishops, in discussing the mission of evangelization today, was to make recommendations leading to more effective programs. From what has been published about the Synod, however, it would seem that while the meeting produced a useful exchange of information and insights, the bishops were unable to arrive at the sort of decisive conclusions that would give present-day evangelization a new orientation.

This work of evangelization cannot be planned as men plan a commercial enterprise. The commitment of faith does not depend on exclusively human efforts as is true of business and other secular spheres of activity. It is always God who ultimately gives the gift of faith, who lets it grow, and who brings it to perfection in those being evangelized.

Such divine activity, while always necessary for effective transmission of the Gospel, does not eliminate the need for careful planning of our efforts or for solid evaluation and discernment of the various options available. On the other hand, our human activity must blend with our efforts to find God's will through prayer. In the Acts of the Apostles, which we might describe as God's own guidelines for authentic evangelization, there is constant emphasis on his direct initiatives in the work of evangelization.

Not only at Pentecost, where the Church was started by a most extraordinary example of divine intervention, but also in the decades that followed, important decisions were often made in harmony with direct and unmistakable interventions by God. Take, for example, Acts 8:26 when Philip was sent to the Ethiopian official, Acts 9:11f when Ananias was ordered to help Saul, Acts 10:19f when Peter was told to evangelize Cornelius, and Acts 16:6-10 when Paul was prevented from continuing his travels in Asia and instead invited to begin the evangelization of Europe.

Such directives from God suppose, of course, a prayerful attitude in the evangelist and a sincere desire to be led by the Holy Spirit in his work. The main difficulty consists in balancing one's own efforts for careful apostolic planning and openness to the Lord's guidance. Men who are inclined to trust their own gifts of decision and organization are usually in danger of not being sufficiently open to divine guidance. Those who wish to depend solely on that guidance too readily dispense themselves from the need for personal effort, and they neglect the prerequisite study and planning.

The authentic evangelist plans his entire work in the light of faith. His study and deliberation of each situation is as solid and careful as that of any businessman. He keeps himself open to God through his daily union with him in prayer, but he leaves to the Lord all decisions as to the method of manifesting his will. People who do not listen to their God-given superiors, who do not seek God's directives in "the signs of the times," or who are not ready to discuss their plans with co-workers in genuine dialogue must not expect that God will render some miraculous guidance for their apostolate. And if they think that they have received such guidance, it will most likely be self-deception.

Today the charismatic renewal is arousing among Christians a new trust in the Spirit of God who has inspired and directed true disciples since that first Pentecost. If we are faithful to the Spirit, he will teach us the proper ways of proclaiming God's dynamic love to modern man. True openness to the Spirit makes Christians ready for new fields of endeavor and new methods of action without immature desires of change merely for the sake of change.

In selecting the opportunities for evangelization that here and now deserve preference, some basic principles can be followed. These principles cannot determine each particular choice but their observance will at least preserve us from many mistakes in our planning.

The evangelist, and especially the professional evangelist, works in the service of God. He is not the master but the servant of those to whom he has been sent. Therefore, he is not supposed to determine his choice of work according to his own preferences but rather by the greater and better service he may render in bringing others closer to God. He is not allowed to lose precious time with people to whom he feels a natural attraction while neglecting others. This principle is self-evident, but its faithful application supposes a high degree of selflessness on the part of the evangelist. Only prayerful union with God can give him the necessary strength.

The word of God is for everyone, for God "wants everyone to be saved and to reach full knowledge of the truth" (1 Tim. 2:4). This loving desire of God cannot be realized by working with small esoteric groups that have little or no impact upon others. Not that working with small groups would be wrong, for intensive work with small groups is indeed indispensable if we hope to penetrate and evangelize the entire community. But the groups chosen must themselves be eager to hand on God's word to others and to serve them in every way.

Since we wish our efforts to be passed on, it is better to concentrate on the evangelization of those with influence, not because they are better people but because through them we can reach others. This is one reason to work intensively for the evangelization of parents; without their support, the evangelization of children is ineffective.

Efforts to interest influential people must, however, never lead us to limit our efforts to the upper classes of society. This would not particularly help them and it would only alienate others. The more influential people in this world, especially in religious matters, are not those with money or high social position, but those who excel by their education, creative abilities, total dedication and generosity, vitality and a natural gift for communicating with others.

In these days we are constantly meeting people who are unbelievers although baptized. There are also a large number of "marginal" Christians who, though they still have some contact with the Church, are desperately in need of thorough re-evangelization. In all probability they have never been evangelized. But how can we evangelize them? And who can do it?

Most present-day unbelievers and marginal Christians are not disposed to accept any direct evangelization, least of all from a priest. And even if they were ready to accept priestly evangelization, most priests could not provide it, since they are already overloaded with the pastoral care of the faithful and thus cannot find the time for the lengthy pre-evangelization that is necessary in most cases.

The most realistic solution here is concentration by the priest-evangelist on the formation of many dedicated and well-trained lay evangelists, both as individuals and in groups. In training them, however, the priest must carefully avoid the old error that lay evangelists are more or less a substitute for priestly ones, providing an emergency solution to a problem caused by the lack of priests.

The outstanding missionary dynamism and success of the early Church resulted, above all, from the missionary spirit of ordinary Christians. They simply could not keep silent about the Good News that had brought so much joy and new meaning into their lives.

Only in the light of the foregoing principles can we correctly evaluate and use the opportunities we are now to ponder in the next section.

Some Outstanding Opportunities for Evangelization

The title of this section makes it clear that we are not attempting any complete list of the various opportunities. The examples we give are a few of the many that could serve equally well in the work of evangelization. We are concerned primarily with showing what ultimately makes such opportunities valid and how they may be used. Also, the sequence with which we mention various possibilities is not meant to establish any rank or preference.

We mention *retreats* first because they may be considered as typical examples of intensive evangelization. In a retreat, each retreatant is helped and invited to prayerful reflection upon his life in the light of God's loving plan for him A good retreat always presents the core of the Christian message in one way or another but is suitably adapted to the particular situation and needs of the retreatants. It always aims at a reform of life or, in other words, at a thorough conversion in the sense of further progress in the service of God. Everything is geared to arouse, motivate and strengthen the basic Christian commitment.

The evangelizing power of a good retreat consists primarily in the way it leads to an existential confrontation with the Good News. The Gospel is experienced as a personal invitation from God extended to us through Jesus Christ. In the dialogue of prayer, Christ challenges the retreatant in his particular situation here and now to a complete surrender and demands from him the determined commitment to faithful fellowship.

In an authentic retreat, God's initiative in calling, guiding and strengthening man, and man's active role in seeking God's will, accepting his call and commiting himself to him, are given due emphasis. The evangelist, here the retreat director, must remain in the background in keeping with his role as intermediary. He does not present his own doctrine but helps the retreatant to listen to God, to ponder his call, and to avoid misinterpretation of God's intention.

By challenging man to an unconditional surrender to Christ and a generous imitation of his life, retreats have, in fact, formed countless dedicated Christians and legions of true apostles. However, one cannot deny that the classical retreats of old had a tendency to overstress the individual aspect of Christian spirituality and did not do full justice to the social and sacramental dimensions.

By unduly shortening retreats—for example, the thirty-day Spiritual Exercises of St. Ignatius Loyola—much of their initial potential has been lost. Especially in our modern era of advanced secularization with all its distractions and impediments to concentration, retreats of weekend length can hardly be expected to yield the remarkable spiritual fruits they achieved with previous generations.

In many ways similar to the shorter retreats are the courses of spiritual training known as "cursillos" after the original Spanish name, *cursillos de cristianidad.* They differ from the ordinary short retreats by making full use of group dynamics and by their purposeful orientation to active participation in the apostolate of the Church. The climax of a good cursillo must be an act of full surrender to Christ that includes a firm determination to be at his disposal in the building up of God's Kingdom here on earth.

Cursillos seem to work best with people who have a basic, although often still dormant faith and who are sufficiently susceptible to the emotional and social dimensions of religion. These are evaluated and used as powerful awakenings of the latent faith. However, cursillos can only give a first push; in order to produce permanent fruits, they are meant to be followed by regular meetings known as "ultreyas," which provide the necessary assistance for the further deepening of faith.

In the cursillos we have classic proof once again of the basic principle that an initial evangelization will not be effective

unless it is continued and further deepened by evangelizing catechesis and pastoral care. Cursillos, incidentally, can be used
with great success for the formation of basic communities which
we shall describe later.

Marvelous apostolic work has been done in the last decades
throughout the world by members of the *Legion of Mary*. Many
legionaries excel by their apostolic skill and dedication. Their
work is inspired by the prayer that is an integral part of all their
meetings, and their methods makes them apt for all phases of
the apostolate that require common sense and dedication. The
Legion's system of planning work in common and of regular
follow-up reports on work already completed has decided ad-
vantages. From the viewpoint of evangelization, however, it can
be regretted that members often lack the necessary training for a
more meaningful contribution to this work. One may also
express some doubts about the quality of the spirituality they
profess and promote. Is it too devotional? Does it need a
thorough updating in the spirit of the Scriptures, the liturgy and
Vatican II? Without such updating there is great danger that
the apostolic contribution of the Legion will decrease in the
years to come.

The regular meetings of the Legion of Mary could be easily
utilized for the evangelization of members so that they could
contribute more effectively to the evangelization of others. With
more formation, legionaries could become excellent evangelists
and bring the basic Gospel message to innumerable homes. The
clergy uses Legion members for all kinds of service within the
Christian community. But is the clergy equally eager to provide
them with the necessary spiritual and catechetical formation?

One of the great hopes of today's Church is the return to
prayer being manifested within the *charismatic renewal*. Many
Christians have here experienced a new desire for prayerful
union with God, and, moved by the Holy Spirit, they gather in
prayer groups. The aim of the charismatic movement is to
renew within the Christian community the spirit, experience and
life of the first followers of Christ and to bring about a new
Pentecost within the Church.

To the extent that this movement is truly "Pentecostal," it

must thoroughly evangelize those who regularly participate in the prayer meetings. It must transform them into true evangelists according to their state of life. The first Pentecostals were surely not just an enthusiastic prayer group but the community of the risen Lord. They felt themselves called by him to a new way of life and were eager to share this experience of new life with others. That made them excellent evangelists.

In any new, dynamic movement there is often a tendency to exaggerations and extravagant claims and even to doctrinal errors. A movement should be judged, however, by the attitude of its leaders and by its effects on the lives of the vast majority of its followers. There is definitely a danger that a good number of charismatics are still too content with emotional expressions of their religious feelings and are failing to give sufficient time and thought to the various tasks awaiting the Christian community. But the responsible leaders of the charismatic renewal are aware of this danger and are trying to meet it. Considering the tremendous potential of the charismatic movement, especially in the sphere of evangelization, one could wish for more active interest and assistance on the part of priests.

The more the secularization of modern society progresses —and it will surely make further progress—the more imperative is pastoral work by small but thoroughly committed groups. In the former monolithic structures of our society, it was different. Public life was entirely shaped by Christian thought and a Christian outlook on life, and it was normal and easy to live an ordinary Christian life.

Today it is certainly not easy, provided one understands that a Christian life is something more than retaining a few traditional customs. In order to be supported in their faith and in their practice of a Christian life-style, believers today need to come together in small groups. Often these are called *basic communities*, a term that originated in Hispanic countries.

Only if such communities are small, comprising no more than about ten couples, can they fulfill their purpose. It is not enough, however, that these groups come together in regular formal meetings. What seems to matter even more is a close union of the lives and activities of all the members, animated by a true spirit of Christian brotherhood.

The last Synod of Bishops gave us a pertinent description of these basic communities. Their characteristics are these: they must form a community of faith in prayer and fraternal charity in action, they must participate together in the word of God and in the Eucharist, and they must give witness to an authentic Christian life by their participation in both the civil society and the ecclesial life of the parish and diocese.

The formation of such basic communities is vitally important for effective re-evangelization of our parishes. But without thorough evangelization, such communities will not be built, for their life and activities require an ongoing process of formation.

Such basic units are intended to serve as leaven for the larger community, the parish. But in order to make this ideal a reality, intensive interest on the part of ecclesial leaders is imperative. If such interest is lacking, such small groups will form anyway, but they will invariably turn against the institutional Church and become a hindrance to evangelization. This was the meaning of the realistic and pertinent remarks about small communities made by the Holy Father at the conclusion of the last Synod and reported in *Osservatore Romano*.

The particular forms of each community's life will vary enormously according to different situations. But independent of these variations, there remains a basic principle for any authentic evangelization. The proclamation of the Gospel is, after all, the action of the Christian community, and it must lead to Christian life within that community. Genuine Christianity was ecclesial from the very beginning.

Evangelization means proclamation and therefore communication, and it has always been necessary to use whatever means of communication are current. Today this means intensive use of the mass media. Many people had hoped that the last Synod of Bishops would give concrete directives in this regard, especially since the preparatory text had emphasized this point and prepared some pertinent questions (*The Evangelization of the Modern World*, Washington 1973, pp. 17f). However, the Synod contents itself with simply acknowledging the great importance of the mass media without giving any detailed directives for its use.

The question is, in fact, much more complicated than many people suspect. It is, for example, very easy to show the tremendous influence of television in creating public opinion, in spreading new ideas, and in molding the mentality of modern man. However, that does not mean that television can be easily adapted for purposes of genuine evangelization.

Three important questions seem to be involved here: (1) What can be done to diminish the bad influences which the mass media often exert? (2) How can the mass media be used to present information about Christianity in the sense of solid pre-evangelization? (3) In what ways can the media, especially television, be used for evangelization in the strict sense and what would be required of such television programs?

What makes the answers difficult is the fact that, until now, those who understood something about evangelization usually knew very little of the mass media and, conversely, media experts were rarely well acquainted with the content and psychology of faith. The dynamics of faith are indeed very different from the dynamics of profane information, entertainment and advertising. The problem probably will not be solved by letting a priest study the psychology and techniques of mass communication, unless he has also been formed in the art of evangelization.

We should never forget that the gift of evangelization is a precious charism. It cannot be learned like a trade. Yet man can and must prepare himself for it. It is always given in some degree with mature faith, and to a large extent it can be obtained by sincere prayer, assuming efforts are also made to study the word of God and to learn the art of human communication.

A true evangelist will find countless opportunities to sow the seed of the Gospel, knowing full well that the vast majority of seeds will bear little or no fruit. A Christian mother of deep faith and solid piety evangelizes best by innumerable daily actions and brief comments which, because they all reveal the same basic orientation of life to God, recommend themselves to those she meets. How much priests could learn from such a mother in their priestly evangelization of others.

Chapter Eleven
Evangelization and Catechesis of Children

The catechesis of children holds a very special place in the process of evangelization. If evangelization is taken in the sense of leading unbelievers to a first commitment to Christ, then catechesis of children cannot be considered as evangelization. Christian children are not unbelievers. With the natural readiness of their age, they accept gradual initiation into the full life of faith. They already have a faithful attitude insofar as they accept the word of God with a ready heart, but at the same time they are not yet, because of their youth, capable of making a commitment of faith in the strict sense.

The case is different if we take the term evangelization in the broader meaning—"proclaiming the Gospel so that faith may be aroused, may unfold and may grow"—that was laid down by the Synod of Bishops. Then catechesis of children obviously is a major part of the whole work of evangelization, even though they are not yet ready to reach a mature faith.

In the past, it is true, we expected too much from the catechesis of children, which, in spite of all the emphasis placed upon it, was rather poorly done. Today we recognize that the problem of evangelization cannot be solved simply by catechesis of children, even where that catechesis is excellent. At the same time, we see clearly the important role such catechesis must play in the overall process of evangelization.

The Evangelizing Task of Children's Catechesis

The place held by catechesis of children in the work of evangelization can be best understood by some simple reflection upon the intent of such catechesis. The children who receive it were baptized while still incapable of any commitment to a Christian life, yet baptism by its very nature requires such commitment. In the case of infant baptism, we encounter a special privilege which God gives to Christian parents and which the Church has recognized since the time of the apostles. Infants may be baptized and thus become children of God as soon as they are born, but only upon the condition that their parents commit themselves to lead these children step-by-step to the Christian commitment they were themselves unable to make at the reception of the sacrament.

Catechesis of children in all of its forms—in the family, parish and school alike—is intended to help children to understand and appreciate the special love of God they received as infants and to respond to this love by a Christian life arising from their own commitment. Such a commitment cannot be made before adolescence because children are too young to make it; they still lack the natural maturity necessary for true and full commitment. It is for this reason that religious education which terminates with First Communion at the age of eight or nine years is essentially deficient and does not fulfill the promises parents make at their child's baptism.

Provided that one accepts these theological principles—and they give the only solid justification for infant baptism—the evangelizing function involved in children's catechesis can be easily understood. It is by means of this catechesis that the first actual faith of the child is aroused and step by step is brought to maturity.

What matters most in this catechesis is not the abstract knowledge of religious doctrines and principles but an existential acceptance of the Gospel that enables the children to live as fully committed Christians. Obviously, a definite knowledge of one's religion is also required but this knowledge is not an end in itself; it is a necessary condition for making the commitment reasonable and firm.

Too often in the past we trusted—without justification—in the "infused" faith that children receive in baptism, and this has been misleading. It cannot be proved that such infused faith gives children any psychological readiness to believe that is lacking in unbaptized children. Infused faith is not in any way a valid substitute for actual faith which has to be aroused and gradually deepened in baptized children.

Any true evangelization must lead those being evangelized to an ever more mature faith. According to the General Catechetical Directory, this maturation of faith includes two aspects: growth in personal adherence to God and progress in religious knowledge (no. 36). In the past, we now recognize, we too often stressed the material aspect—religious knowledge—to the detriment of the formal aspect—the commitment of faith.

Such overemphasis upon the doctrinal aspect, especially in school catechesis, usually did little harm as long as the religious education within the family put great emphasis on the personal adherence to God. The disastrous consequences of such imbalance became much more evident as families began to fail in their educational task. Children who had been through an intensive catechesis of eight or more years came to the end of this program with little interest in religion and less committed than they were at the time of their First Communion. Such situations are not always, it is true, the result of defective catechesis, but usually this is at least partially responsible.

If we hope to solidly evangelize the upcoming generation, we will have to insist not only on the evangelizing aspect of catechesis but also on its continuation until the end of adolescence. In many places there is now an alarming lack of catechetical care for adolescents and young adults. Thus we can readily understand the need for special care for this age group without delay. At the same time, we must remember that one of the chief reasons for the difficulties of these young people is precisely our neglect of the evangelizing aspect when they were younger.

The following comparison may help to clarify what I say. The formation of good doctors, as everyone agrees, requires solid medical studies at the university level. It cannot be achieved through excellent teaching at the primary and secondary levels. But a neglect at the primary and secondary education levels will make studies at the college level impossible.

In exceptional cases, the lack of a solid primary and secondary education may be compensated by the special efforts of individual students, but such exceptions serve only to confirm the rule. Especially in today's thoroughly secularized world, we cannot hope to evangelize the great mass of adolescents and young adults if we neglect the catechesis of children.

How To Accomplish the Catechesis of Children

Although we cannot expect mature faith from children, we can at least prepare them to achieve maturity later. Such maturation is a long process which in a normal case of Christian life is supposed to start in childhood. Here we must equally avoid two extremes.

On the one hand, we must avoid all exaggerated demands by requiring more of children than they can achieve at their age. Such demands sooner or later almost always lead to dangerous crises in religious or moral life.

On the other hand we must take advantage of the great and genuine religious capacity of children and lead them, as they are able, to a deep and sincere adherence to God in preparation for later commitment. We must avoid the great error of assuming that their youth allows us to content ourselves with the mere external expression of faith on their part. Despite their immaturity, children have a marvelous capacity for systematic development of a solid interior adherence to God.

In order to make the catechesis of children a genuine evangelization, the following points deserve special consideration.

1. The first thing needed is *proper appreciation* of catechesis on the part of parents. Many parents give their children practically no religious training within the family. When they send them to Catholic schools or to parish religion programs, they do it primarily in the hope that such education will make the children more submissive and manageable at home. What such parents really appreciate is not religion as such but its

hoped-for by-product. They are doing exactly the same thing within their "kingdoms" as did many monarchs of old who, without taking religion seriously themselves, favored religious education for their subjects in order to protect their thrones. They lost them and they deserved to lose them.

One of the main reasons why catechesis is so often unsatisfactory is precisely the lack of collaboration on the part of the family. In order to make our religion program effective, we must insist on their indispensable cooperation.

Children whose parents fail to show a minimum interest and desire for collaboration should not be accepted. We can be sorry for them, but we must admit realistically that accepting them would not solve their problems and would only hamper our work with the others. Parents who never come to a meeting with the religion teachers in the school or parish do not manifest the necessary interest on their part.

We also must sincerely face the evidence that in a good many schools and church education programs today, religious education is not being given the emphasis and appreciation it needs if we are to form true Christians. True evangelization can be accomplished even within a secularized environment, but it must involve a profound awareness and appreciation of specific Christian values that have little place in our present world and that faith alone can contribute. We should not expect much in the way of worthwhile evangelizing results if we do not incorporate an existential approach into our presentation of the Gospel.

2. Children cannot yet fully understand the greatness and depth of God's saving plan in the same way that adults are supposed to understand them, but that does not justify a lack of proper presentation of the essential facts of the Christian religion. Rather, the catechesis of children must be distinguished by its *concentration on the main elements* of Christ's message presented in such a way that they can comprehend the constant emphasis on God's loving intention to call us to a great and happy life with him.

One of the most common shortcomings in the catechesis of children consists in presenting prematurely and indiscriminately too many religious elements and not integrating them properly into the central theme of God's love. From the very beginning, the Christian message must be presented to them in such a way that they really grasp and experience it as joyful tidings, as good news. Whatever cannot be taught lucidly in the light of God's love and our response of love to love has no place in the catechesis of children.

3. In order to make the religion program authentic evangelization, it is not enough to present or live some impersonal Christian virtues. True evangelization *leads to Christ himself* and with him to God as our Lord and Father. This personal relationship with Christ as our divine brother, Lord and Savior must be the focal point of all our catechetical efforts. We succeed with the evangelization of youngsters to the extent that Christ retains an ever more important role in their lives. For psychological reasons, this personal approach is even more important with young people than with adults.

4. Any catechesis that truly evangelizes must place great stress on *guidance to personal prayer*, inasmuch as prayer, more than anything else, expresses and actualizes our loving adherence to God. This is of particular importance in the catechesis of children. Mechanical prayers, however, are useless—they hinder more than they help. But to think that children are still incapable of true personal prayer is a great error.

Much, of course, depends upon the way in which we familiarize children with God's love and upon our guidance in encouraging them to pray. Needless to say, only an educator who appreciates prayer and prays often himself can teach the art of prayer to others.

Two common shortcomings in the sphere of prayer are excessive emphasis on ready-made formulas and the lack of adaptations to the age of the children being taught. Unfortunately, many educators fail to distinguish between well-adapted, valuable prayers and childish, sentimental ones that lack value for children and adults alike.

5. Although catechesis has far more as its aim than an appropriate preparation for *First Communion and Confession*, these two sacraments must have a prominent place. Through

these sacraments, children must learn that their reception requires a sincere commitment. When children receive them for the first time, they may still be incapable of making a mature commitment, but that does not dispense them from the necessity of an initial commitment according to their capability.

We must make certain that the doctrine that the sacraments produce their effect *ex opere operato* is correctly understood. Otherwise, there is a danger of harmful sacramentalism. To consider the sacraments or to use them in any way as substitutes for the commitment of faith contradicts the Gospel and is in opposition to authentic evangelization, which puts the emphasis on the commitment of faith. (This has already been discussed in Chapter Six.)

Solid eucharistic education must encourage children toward ever more committed participation in the Eucharist. In the past, we tended to overstress the reception of First Communion and badly neglected, at times, the importance of continuing growth in eucharistic life. Mere mechanical attendance at Mass is of questionable value and, especially today, may generate an attitude of resentment that eventually provokes a total break with the life of the Church.

It is not an easy task to lead children step-by-step to a more conscious participation in the Eucharist, but this does not dispense us from the necessity of making every effort to achieve it. It is, above all, in the celebration of the Eucharist that the mature Christian asserts his Christian vocation and renews and deepens his Christian commitment. We cannot expect all this from children, but we must help them to learn that it should be part of their adult life.

As with the eucharistic life, so also with the attitude of true loving repentance. It must be gradually deepened as children grow in other ways. No one can truly repent without renewing and deepening his Christian commitment. Is not this the aim of all evangelization worthy of the name?

6. Evangelizing catechesis in all its forms is marked by *an insistence upon the Christian life* as a response to God's loving invitation. The catechesis of children, especially within the school, can run the risk of putting too much emphasis on the in-

tellectual aspects of religious education. Many children resent religion and stop practicing it if they are subjected to an overly "scholarly" catechesis that has no direct contact with Christian life. The result of such catechesis is the direct opposite of true evangelization.

Whenever religion is being taught as an integral part of the school curriculum, care must be taken to insure that the pupils clearly realize it is different from other subjects. This distinction must affect the whole atmosphere of the religion class, the manner of examination and grading, and especially the close relationship of the subject with the personal life of the students. Whatever is being taught and learned must be clearly related to life. When students look upon religion instruction as just one more subject in the curriculum, it fails to evangelize.

Yet proper emphasis on the Christian life and the practice of religion should not imply premature participation of small children in the prayer life of the family or the ecclesial community. Such premature participation not only disturbs the prayer of others but, even worse, leads to formalistic religiosity. They become accustomed to mere exterior participation in their pre-school years, which is just what true evangelization strives to eliminate.

7. Evangelization must lead to a mature and authentic faith. A catechesis of high evangelizing quality cannot, therefore, be expected from educators who themselves are not deeply rooted in faith or who lack the necessary formation. If we are determined to provide our children with true evangelizing catechesis, *the careful selection and solid formation* of the catechist is indispensable.

A catechetical formation aimed at preparing true "evangelists" must put great emphasis on *spiritual formation*. Until now this formation has often been lacking in otherwise excellent and updated training programs. Only spiritual men and women can lead others to living and joyful faith.

8. Pastoral experience provides abundant evidence that catechesis in school and parish had meager results *without the collaboration of the family*. The intellectual dimension of religious education can easily be developed through catechesis in

school or parish, provided that the family shows interest and concern for the foundation of faith and its gradual growth. But without this contribution from the family, school and parish labor in vain. A better, more intensive collaboration between parents and catechists is one of the most urgent demands in the field of religious education.

One great difficulty is the obvious fact that many parents do not give their children any home religious training worthy of the name. Or else, parents may still be passing down a traditional piety that is too devotional and ritualistic. The present generation does not respond to such instruction. Many parents do not lack good will, but rather the formation necessary to understand and fulfill their all-important task.

Our work must include helping such parents to live up to their own responsibilities as religious educators. The best religion texts today all try to involve parents in the religious instruction that their children receive from the school or parish, and these have proved very helpful.

Much greater efforts on the part of parishes and their leaders are needed, however. The English-speaking world could well use something similar to the *catequesis familiar* (family catechesis) program in use in Mexico. This program is being propagated primarily by the Basilian Fathers who went to Mexico from the United States and Canada. (For further information, write to: Padres Basilianos, Apdo. 9, Tehuacan, Pue., Mexico.)

Chapter Twelve
Obstacles to Evangelization

Although there may be no lack of opportunities for evangelization in the world today, there are many obstacles that impede it. Here we will first consider some of the attitudes that contradict the spirit of evangelization and hinder it. After this, we will deal with some situations which render evangelization difficult and at times even impossible.

Improper Attitudes

The following attitudes may be found in those who evangelize or in those to be evangelized; they inevitably impede evangelization and not infrequently make it entirely ineffective.

1. *Traditionalism.* The obstacles presented by traditionalism do not, of course, consist in the acceptance and appreciation of the valuable religious heritage handed down to us by former generations. Such acceptance and appreciation are obviously good and desirable. Rather, the problem lies in blind acceptance of former practices without the necessary discernment and adaptation for today's life situations.

In the same measure that blind acceptance substitutes for solid motives justifying the commitment of faith, traditionalism contradicts the nature of evangelization, that is, the growth to mature faith. The General Catechetical Directory denounces this traditionalism and in its place recommends authentic re-evangelization: "The question now is not one of merely preserving traditional religious customs, but rather of fostering an appropriate re-evangelization of men, obtaining their reconversion and giving them a deeper and more mature education in faith" (no. 6).

When we evangelize people and especially whole congregations that suffer from undue traditionalism, we have need for great pastoral discretion, prudence and patience. In such a situation, we must never begin with harsh criticism of the traditions, but rather with the positive creation of new attitudes that justify the necessary and proper changes.

Obstinate traditionalism is not going to be remedied by an immature revolutionary attitude that employs much the same blindness in desiring to change everything just for the sake of change. Even in the case of unreasonable traditionalism, people have a right to expect that we will respect their sincere religious convictions and avoid all offensive sarcasm.

2. *Intellectualism.* This obstacle does not lie in denying or impeding the important and indispensable role of the intellect in a meaningful life of faith. The pitfall lies in the tendency to consider divine revelation as information about God and godly things, rather than as God's loving invitation to man to respond in faith and love. Catechesis which only informs and does not seriously prepare, call forth and deepen the commitment of faith and love simply loses its evangelic character. This important point has already been stressed in Chapters One Two and Ten and needs no further discussion here.

3. *Pessimism.* The problem here does not consist in a presentation of man and his world as they really are without glossing over his limitations and faults. This cannot be avoided if catechesis is to be realistic and useful. As Christians, we do not favor childish, untrue optimism, for we know our Gospel is meant for sinful man.

But the main thrust of our message must always rest upon Christ, who is the unshakable foundation of all our hopes because he has overcome sin and death. A sad, pessimistic attitude contradicts the very nature of evangelism. A message which does not lead to deep and permanent joy, full of hope and love, is simply not "good news."

This joyful, optimistic attitude must characterize all catechetical activity. The more faith and love grow, the more fear vanishes. "There is no fear in love; perfect love drives out all fear. So, then, love has not been made perfect in the one who fears" (1 Jn. 4:18). Catechists who are sad and austere—pessimists and rigorists—are bad "evangelists." They do not live and represent the Gospel they preach, and therefore they lack credibility.

4. *Ritualism.* This obstacle obviously does not consist in the appreciation and use of the exterior elements of religion. If God created man, his masterpiece, as a body-person, the body must have an indispensable part to play in man's total dedication and service of God. Religious psychology has shown that a reasonable and balanced use of the exterior elements of religion —rites, gestures, formulas, etc.—facilitates and perfects man's union with the divine.

The exterior elements thus are invaluable aids to express and deepen religious commitment properly. However, any tendency to substitute the exterior action, sacramental or not, for the interior commitment always contradicts the Gospel and hinders true evangelization. Religious psychology rightly insists that an excessive amount of exterior rites, such as we so often find in unenlightened popular religion, leads invariably to morbid ritualism.

The worst form of ritualism—the one most opposed to the Gospel—is religious commercialism. Here, the ritualism of ordinary people, out of more or less disguised motives, is promoted or at least tolerated passively for the sake of material profit.

5. *Legalism.* This obstacle does not consist in assigning to the juridical aspect its proper place in institutionalized religion. If God in his love decided to save us within and through a saving community, institutional elements cannot be eliminated or simply disregarded. Even our relationship with God himself includes elements of the juridical order, although on a higher level.

Our relationship of love with God does not annul his supreme claims as Creator and Lord. Yet, any undue emphasis on these "juridical" aspects contradicts the Gospel. Through that Gospel Christ intends man to establish a relationship of deepest friendship with God and a brotherhood of love with all men. By so doing, Jesus challenged the legalism of the Pharisees of his time.

True evangelism aims to lead men more and more to a loving surrender of himself to the God of our Lord Jesus Christ who revealed himself as love. With a religious attitude that is, in fact, more concerned with the letter of the law than with the law's Author, we cannot approach the God of love.

A legalistic attitude easily infects catechesis about the Christian way of life. The herald of the Gospel must present clearly and with the necessary emphasis the main obligations of a truly Christian life. But what is even more important than the explanation of the various Christian duties is the building up of the fundamental Christian attitude. And that is an attitude of love, not of fear.

The most characteristic question in a life of true love is not "What must I do?" but rather "What can I do in order to please the Beloved One?" In his own teaching, especially as we find it presented in the Sermon on the Mount, Christ put all of his emphasis on the basic attitude of total surrender to God (see, e.g., Mt. 5:3; 6:24; 22:37-40). Was Christ a good catechist?

6. *Devotionalism*. This obstacle is not the recommending and using of particular devotions—for example, Marian devotion—in the process of religious education. Popular devotions can be of great help if used properly. What hinders evangelization is a surfeit of popular devotions. The function of devotions in the Christian life is similar to that of condiments in our food. A discreet use of them definitely helps us to eat more substantial food and to eat it with more relish. But as soon as we overindulge in them, they injure our health and can almost become poison.

True evangelism puts its emphasis on the core of the Christian message: the love of God who has called us through his Son and made us his very own children by giving us his Spirit. The sincere acceptance of this Gospel leads us by inner necessity to the Christian prayer by which we in union with Christ respond to the love of the Father: "Abba, my Father" (Gal. 4:6; Rom. 8:15). Only in the Holy Spirit can we pray this way.

This fundamental form of genuine Christian prayer must be increasingly deepened throughout the whole process of religious growth. In the liturgy we know we are united with our heavenly brothers and sisters. We admire them as the most noble members of the mystical body.

The main thrust of the liturgy, however, is always the same: through Jesus Christ we approach God our heavenly Father in the Holy Spirit. In the liturgy we pray always with the saints but only rarely to them. The reason why any overemphasis on particular devotions hinders true evangelism is obvious. Evangelization must lead to an ever deeper appreciation of the center of Christian religion, and devotionalism diverts attention from the center to the periphery.

Devotionalism, in the pejorative sense, is also characterized by excessive emphasis on the emotional aspects of religion. Sentiments have, of course, an important part in genuine prayer and in authentic Christian life. The main stress, however, must always be put upon the sincere, firm commitment of faith and love, which does not waver and is independent of momentary feelings. Emotion can never substitute for such commitment.

7. *Secularism.* Here the obstacle does not involve due appreciation of human values and of this world that God has created for man. The necessary integration of temporary values into our preaching of the Gospel has already been dealt with in Chapter Eight. But secularism in the sense of worldliness is something different; it consists in harmful overemphasis on temporal values and on the secular activity of man.

Undeniably pre-conciliar catechesis frequently did not do justice to temporal values and their role in God's plan of salvation, but this does not give us any right to go to the other extreme now. No one can deny that today's "evangelists" face greater danger from secularism than from devotionalism.

Unfavorable Situations

In addition to the attitudes which we have just described, there are many situations that hinder effective evangelization. The following situations seem to deserve special attention.

1. *Misery.* When we speak of obstacles to evangelization, misery must clearly be distinguished from poverty. One of the

characteristics of messianic evangelization is precisely the preaching of the Gospel to the poor (Mt. 11:5; Lk. 4:18). Christ congratulates the poor (Mt. 5:3; Lk. 6:32) because they have a special chance to enter the Kingdom of God.

In the early Church a large majority of the Christians were poor and lowly people (see, e.g., 1 Cor. 1:26; 2 Cor. 8:2; Jas. 2:5; Rev. 2:9). The poor are those who must toil to obtain what they need to live; they have enough to survive but not enough to enjoy a secure and comfortable life; because of their humble social condition, they often must depend on the good will of the more affluent. Yet all of this does not make them any less capable or open to the loving call of God; quite the contrary, the man who is weak in material things is often more disposed to accept the Good News than his rich and secure neighbor.

In the case of misery, it is quite different. Misery consists in the lack of those material goods necessary to keep man from "vegetating." Misery means hunger and poor housing, it means a lack of clean water, light, sanitation and clothing—in sum, a lack of human dignity. Misery dehumanizes man because it absorbs all his energies in a bare struggle for existence. It depersonalizes and deprives man of hope and natural vigor.

It is precisely because of this depersonalization that misery is an obstacle to evangelization. In fact, the missionary history of the Church shows that misery has been a grave obstacle, although usually it does not make evangelization impossible.

In order to evangelize effectively in situations where misery is present, it is necessary, above all, to instill in those living under such conditions a new experience of their human dignity and to stimulate their hope. At the same time, the evangelist must sympathize profoundly with those in misery and must prove his compassion with something more than empty words or ineffectual sentiments. His compassion must impel him to share as much as he can in the unfortunate lives of his deprived brothers and sisters.

Except in very rare cases, however, and then only for a short time, the work of direct evangelization should not be halted for social service. What people in this situation of misery need most is new meaning in their lives. The testimony of all the great evangelizers is unanimous in this regard.

The principal difficulty with evangelization in a situation of misery is not misery as such, but the problem of recruiting and forming a sufficient number of dedicated evangelists capable of working under such conditions. A Church which is overflowing with words of compassion but which treats people who live on the margins of human society as marginal citizens of the Kingdom of God loses its credibility.

The same is true with regard to the poor. Poverty as such is no obstacle to evangelization, but lack of interest in and identification with the poor does create a serious and rather frequent obstacle. A Church which identifies itself only with the rich and powerful and fails to defend the poor against the exploitation of the rich simply cannot evangelize the poor. What the ordinary man experiences as Church is the local Christian community in which he lives. The universal Church, with its magnificent conciliar documents and social encyclicals, does not impress him at all—or impresses him unfavorably—if the pastor and the local community fail to live the teachings contained in these texts.

2. *Injustice and Oppression.* What we have just said of misery holds equally true in cases of injustice and oppression. They do not hinder evangelization unless the lack is so great that, as with misery, it depersonalizes men. The early Church with great success evangelized the most oppressed class of the time, the slaves.

The Gospel unequivocally condemns any kind of injustice and oppression. Human dignity and personal freedom are among its basic teachings. In a world of great injustice and oppression, the first messengers of the Gospel stressed incessantly that the Lord "does not favor one person more than the other" (Col. 3:25; Acts 10:34; Rom. 2:11; Eph. 6:9; 1 Pet. 1:17) and applied this fundamental rule explicitly to the social order of their times with all its abuses.

There has always been great injustice and oppression requiring condemnation by the Gospel messengers, but modern man is much more sensitive to these conditions than were the men of past generations. Men today experience great difficulty in accepting the evangelization of a Church whose official representatives, out of fear of those in power, do not preach the Kingdom of God and its justice.

However, we must understand that the Church cannot speak out with equal clarity in all circumstances. There have been and are situations where the Church also suffers from unjust oppression and must fight for its very existence. In such cases, it must proclaim clearly the basic principles of social justice, human dignity and freedom in a general way, even if it cannot apply them explicitly to the particular situation. It must, however, avoid all cowardly adulation of the unworthy men who hold power.

The obligation to defend the rights of the poor and the oppressed does not dispense the messenger of the Gospel from the general law of love or from his special duty to bring and to promote peace. He must never instigate hatred but must promote generous efforts for mutual understanding and respect.

3. *Affluence.* His mandate makes the messenger of the Gospel the defender of the poor and the oppressed. If the Gospel message is properly proclaimed, it contributes tremendously to the promotion of peace, prosperity, freedom and justice. As we have seen, conditions of misery, injustice and oppression are obstacles to evangelization and must be removed.

Let us not, however, forget or conceal the fact that according to the Scriptures, affluence constitutes a much more serious obstacle to evangelization and salvation: "I tell you solemnly, it will be hard for the rich man to enter the Kingdom of heaven. Yes, I tell you again; it is easier for a camel to pass through the eye of a needle than for a rich man to enter the kingdom of heaven" (Mt. 19:36f; see also Lk. 16:19-31; 12:15-21). Did the Lord not say this in a situation of evangelization when the rich young man rejected the loving invitation of the Lord? Where in the Scriptures do we find a similar word with regard to the spiritual condition of those who suffer from misery and oppression?

Affluence makes it very difficult for man to preserve his interior freedom in the midst of his riches. Affluence easily deludes man; he no longer perceives his spiritual needs. He lives in a world which easily makes him, as it were, incapable of being evangelized. He already has "everything" he desires.

Some rich people react to their wealth in another dangerous manner. Riches make them powerful, and power makes them proud and deaf to the invitation of the Lord. Others succumb to the enslaving influence of money. The more they possess, the more they want; their hearts harden with regard to God and man alike.

Such spiritual have-nots surely deserve our profound compassion, but they cannot be evangelized effectively by messengers of the Gospel who themselves are fascinated by their riches and are eager to share in their affluence. Only evangelists who enjoy true freedom and find their happiness in the Gospel by a simple but spiritually rich life can serve effectively in such cases.

4. *Bad Example in the Church.* One of the most embarrassing obstacles to evangelization has always been the bad example of the Christian community and some of its leaders. Scandals will always exist, not only in the world but also in the Church. Unfortunately, modern man takes greater offense at the ordinary defects of the Church than did his ancestors in times when the scandals were much greater.

What usually repels men today are not the scandals in the private lives of Church leaders but the shortcomings of the Christian community. It seems to them that the Church of today differs too much from what Christ really intended. We do not intend here to give a list of some of these defects that offend many men today. We all know what they are and how they hinder successful evangelization. We will, instead, give some suggestions as to how to deal with such situations.

In a dialogue with men today, a defensive attitude does not serve any good purpose. We should never try to deny or minimize unduly obvious defects. After all, are we not messengers of the truth?

We should avoid any destructive criticism. There are two very different methods of critique. One depresses and embitters. It does not emanate from love; instead, it always proves the absence of true love. Very often it originates from some disguised effort to escape reform in one's own life.

The other method, on the contrary, is the result of true loving concern for the Church; it purifies and animates, leading to a new life. The scandals in the pilgrim Church sadden the man of faith, but they do not really depress him, and surely they do not paralyze him. "Our faith lets us overcome the world" (1 Jn. 5:4). Above all, faith helps us to overlook and rise above all worldiness within our Church.

The deficiencies of the universal Church and of large sectors of the Church lose their de-evangelizing power to the extent that we are able to lead our brothers and sisters to a deep and authentic experience of Christian life within small communities.

Whoever experiences within such small but fully committed communities the greatness and purity of true Christian existence may still be aware of the scandals within the universal Church, but they will not hinder him very much. The same can be said of individual people. What impresses us is the good or bad example of those who are close to us in daily life. This proves once again the fundamental importance of a truly Christian life within the family or in small groups of fully committed Christians, groups such as the "basic communities."

Chapter Thirteen
We Need a New Pentecost

When I showed the manuscript of the last chapter to a good friend with extensive pastoral experience in North and South America and the Pacific Islands, he advised me to add "laziness" to the list of obstacles to evangelization. This was sound advice, when one considers the many forms of lassitude and indolence that impede evangelization. All of them stem from an attitude decidedly opposed to authentic evangelization with its ardent desire to share the Good News with others.

Tepid Christians and perfunctory clergy do not evangelize. Because of their indolence, they miss the best opportunities for proclaiming the Good News, and even when they do teach religion, it is simply not evangelization. True evangelization supposes religious fervor just as steam supposes some boiling liquid.

This brings us to a decisive point which, in our opinion, did not receive the necessary emphasis at the last Synod of Bishops. There was, of course, a great deal of talk about all of the difficulties that evangelization encounters, and many pertinent observations and helpful suggestions were made.

But did the Synod really make it clear that the main problem is not the difficult, often hostile environment in which the Church finds itself, but rather the undeniable ebb of religious interest and fervor that we see at present throughout vast sectors of that same Church?

We are faced with a widespread relaxation of religious discipline which is really alarming since it results in great part from a lack of living faith. There is also a manifest lack of missionary zeal throughout the Catholic world. Only in times like these could it happen that some missionaries openly question the urgency of proclaiming the Gospel and insist that instead of its direct proclamation, we should give preference to human development.

We deceive ourselves if we think that only young people have lost interest in religion; statistics about the decreasing religious practice of adults show otherwise. What is even more alarming than the sharp decline of practice of many Catholics is the religious attitude of those who still do practice their religion.

There were always a good number of Christians whose religion was more a result of family tradition, environmental influence and opportunism. If such Christians cease their religious practice in times like ours, it should not be surprising. But can we say that those who are still practicing have been deepened in their faith and are in a position to start a deep-rooted religious renewal which could lead to a new golden age of evangelism?

The same must be said with regard to the exodus of the many who have left the priesthood and religious life since the Council, often without any serious attempt to obtain the necessary permission. Church history has no precedent for such an exodus affecting the Church throughout the world. But what is more alarming, it seems to us, is the fact that this exodus until now has not led to a thorough renewal of those who remain.

Whoever considers objectively the present religious situation of the Church must admit that it is critical. This is not to deny the many particular aspects of progress and hope also present today. It only means that the overall picture clearly includes elements of great and acute danger. The Church is moving toward a turning point that could end in an almost universal breakdown.

It cannot be the aim of this present study, and certainly not of its final chapter, to present a thorough analysis of the critical situation we have just sketched. We only wish to insist that the evangelizing power of the Church is critically linked to its religious renewal. It was admittedly the aim of Vatican II to bring about a thorough religious renewal. The Council, to be sure, gave splendid directives, and the post-conciliar period is bringing many valuable improvements in various sections of ecclesial life, but, taken as a whole, the present religious situation cannot be characterized as a successful renewal but rather as a serious crisis.

We can only touch briefly here on the main reasons why the great hopes pinned upon Vatican II were not realized more fully. Too many people expected that others would do the reforming instead of taking upon themselves the pains involved in any deep religious renewal. We discussed too much and prayed too little. Also, quite often we did not give primary consideration to the more important needs.

It is true that the Church needed a thorough updating which had been too long delayed. It definitely needed a thorough rethinking of its place in the modern world. However, it needed even more a deep experience of Christian faith and life in the midst of this increasingly secularized world. Without this deepening of faith the result could only be a secularization of the Church and not a Christianization of the world.

The apostles of the much needed aggiornamento very often acted under the erroneous supposition that if we just "modernized" the Church, everything would be all right. This kind of modernization was disastrous because it lacked the necessary religious depth. Instead of growing, we lost much of our religious dynamism with the inevitable consequence of decreasing interest in and capacity for evangelization.

What we need more than anything else in the present situation is a new Pentecost, a new and deep religious experience of the basic elements of faith and life. It can only be obtained in prayer, but it can renew all sectors of Christian activity. We humbly expect it as an undeserved gift from God's mercy, for we know he will give it if we approach him humbly in prayer and open ourselves to his grace.

This gift of a loving Father begins with a thorough conversion in the spirit of true and therefore loving repentance. It cannot be obtained by manipulation, by mere human planning or skillful organization.

It would be wrong and ungrateful to overlook the fact that such a renewal is already going on in the Church today. However, that renewal is still in its embryonic state; it needs to be deepened and made universal. We find it most clearly in small groups which have with God's grace achieved a new experience of Christian faith and whose members help one another to deepen this God-given insight and power.

Generally speaking, we find the hopeful beginning of true Christian renewal still lacking in many seminaries and religious communities. We also have to admit that it has not yet sufficiently influenced the current professional theology. This causes grave problems, but it does not give us any right to take refuge in hopelessly conservative theology or any kind of shortsighted biblical fundamentalism.

We do not want to identify this revival with the charismatic renewal, but we definitely hope that the charismatic movement will further develop in a healthy way and have an important part within this religious revival. It will be truly Catholic to the measure that it respects and stresses the ecclesiastical dimensions of religious renewal.

Only as the result of such a thorough and healthy religious renewal can we again have a truly evangelizing catechesis. Grounded in deep personal faith, the catechist will then be able to lead his or her listeners to a similar experience of faith. Such catechesis will reverberate with the joy and infectious certainty of genuine faith. It will lead to concentration on the essentials of Christianity with Christ himself at the very center. Resulting from the prayer experience of the catechist, it will lead all those to genuine prayer who, with faith, accept God's loving invitation.

Authentic evangelization and genuine pentecostal experience are inseparably intertwined from their beginnings. Evangelization, as we have tried to comprehend and evaluate it in this study, always supposes the coming of the Holy Spirit first to the "evangelist," leading him to the joyful experience of our salvation through Christ. Only from this "pentecostal" experience can true "preaching in our languages of the great things God has done" (Acts 2:11) come forth. Such preaching is true evangelization.

Index

abnegation of oneself, 111ff., 117
absence of God, 45
adaptation, 26f., 109
adolescents, 12f., 20, 41, 127f.
adults, 13, 127
affluence, 141f.
aggiornamento, 1, 146
Americans, 27
Ananias, 116
apostles, 5
ascetism, 111
Augustine, Saint, 33f.

bad examples within the Church, 142f.
baptism, close connection with evangelization, 6, 62f.
baptism of infants, 69ff., 76, 126f.
basic communities, 13, 122f., 143; *see also* small groups
Basilian Fathers, 133
Bible, 29, 110
bishops, 106
books, 102

catechesis of adolescents, 13, 41, 127f.
catechesis of children, 9, 104, 125-133
catechesis and evangelization, 7-11
catechesis proper, 7ff.
catechetical renewal, 1
catechist, *see* evangelist
catequesis familiar, 133
Catholic schools, 70, 128-133
celebration of sacraments, 75

central idea of the Christian message, *see* core
centralism, 113
challenge of the Christian message, 57f.
charismatic renewal, 117, 121f., 147
children, evangelization of, 125-133
Christ, calls to conversion, 30; center of the Christian message, 54f., 58, 135, 147; emphasizes the interior, 67; place in evangelization, 3f., 58, 128; *see also* content, eucharist, mystery of Christ, core of the Christian message, paschal mystery, salvation
Christ event, core of apostolic evangelization, 54
Church, committed community, 56f., 61; communion, 56; community of the risen Lord, 56f., 122; concerned with the temporal order, 96; confraternity of love and prayer, 56, 62; does not produce the Gospel, 50; institution, 70f.; missionary dynamism of the ancient Church, 116f.; pentecostal experience, 56; people of the New Covenant, 55f.; place in the core of the Christian message, 56f.; place in the modern world, 146; primitive Christian community, 63; structured from the beginning, 56, 123; *see also* ecclesial

148